D1066297

ILLUSIONS OF OUR CULTURE

By the same author:

Published by Hodder and Stoughton, Harpers and the Ryerson Press:

BARRIERS TO CHRISTIAN BELIEF

THE ETERNAL LEGACY

THE CRUCIAL ENCOUNTER

Published by Hodder and Stoughton and Word Inc.:

GOD IN MAN'S EXPERIENCE

Published by the Lutterworth Press, the Abingdon Press and the Ryerson Press:

GOD AND HIS PEOPLE

THE ROMAN LETTER TODAY

BENEATH THE CROSS OF JESUS

WHAT IS A CHRISTIAN?

GOD'S TIME AND OURS

THIS IS LIVING

Published by the Independent Press and the Abingdon Press:

PATHWAYS TO HAPPINESS

ILLUSIONS OF OUR CULTURE

by

LEONARD GRIFFITH

WORD BOOKS PUBLISHER
WACO, TEXAS

First printed in 1969

First American edition—June 1970

Second American edition—January 1971

SBN 340 10713 8

Printed in the United States of America

In appreciation and friendship
I dedicate this book to
a distinguished American

ROBERT DOUGLAS STUART

Industrialist - Diplomat - Christian

A man with no illusions

AUTHOR'S PREFACE

Fifteen years ago in his Lyman Beecher Lectures on Preaching, given at Yale University, Halford Luccock declared, "What a theme for the preacher, the illusions of our culture!" The phrase has haunted me ever since. As a preacher, and therefore as an interpreter of God's Word to the human situation, I have tried to study and understand not only the situation itself but also its interpretation in the world of thought which we call our "culture".

I am concerned by the fact that our culture is shot through with illusions which, if they are believed, will endanger society and deprive the individual of self-fulfilment. The reason for their presence is that so many of the spokesmen of our culture—broadcasters, lecturers, writers, editors, poets, philosophers and artists—are not men of deep religious faith.

In 1969 a religious journal in Canada conducted a nationwide opinion poll to discover the names of the mass media communicators who exercise the greatest influence on popular thinking. The people named were invited to answer questionnaires telling what they believe about the purpose of life, about God, about the Church. Of the fourteen who replied, four claimed affiliation with the Church, four described themselves as humanist, four as agnostic. Here are some of their answers: "I define God as my conscience." "Jesus was a well-intentioned man, one of the world's great optimists." "The reason for mankind's existence is to exist." "The effect of religion on man has been to keep him in line through fear of the unknown." "After death there is nothing."

Illusions! But what frightens me is that any one of these spokesmen of our culture, however illusory his ideas, exercises a greater influence on popular thought than do all the spokesmen of God put together. Obviously, the Church is no longer a match for them. Yet the Word of God must still be spoken, the Word Incarnate in Jesus and contained in the Scriptures that bear witness to him. That Word is real, and no illusion can permanently survive in its presence.

Out of my concern came the series of sermons which are published in this book. I thank the office secretaries of Deer Park Church who prepared the manuscript; Mr. Charles Reid (once of Eastbourne) who read the proofs; and Mr. Edward England, Religious Editor of Hodder and Stoughton, who encouraged and guided me from the beginning. I offer these chapters with gratitude to all who have enriched their thought and in the hope that they will commend the truth of the Gospel to many readers within and beyond the bounds of the visible Church.

LEONARD GRIFFITH.

Toronto, Canada,
Lent, 1969

CONTENTS

CHAPTER 1

THE ILLUSION OF AFFLUENCE

The phrase "illusions of our culture" occurs in the writings of Tertullian, one of the early Church Fathers, when he speaks of "men already civilized and under the illusions of their very culture". Every civilization has nursed its own pet illusions—for example, about the Roman Empire lasting for ever, about the earth being the centre of the universe, about war being the most decisive means of settling human disputes. Invariably these illusions are reflected in man's culture, that is, in man's way of interpreting his own situation—in his philosophies, his systems of education, his music, art, literature, journalism and amusements. What makes them illusory is that while they seem to be true they are actually false. They have the appearance of reality but no more substance than the cooling springs and leafy trees of a desert mirage. Some cynics place religion in that category, but the truth is that religion has always been a supremely *dis*illusioning force in human life and society. The prophets of Israel were the bubble-bursters of their age. Jesus directed a large part of his teaching ministry to puncturing the popular illusions of his day.

One of the great illusions of our culture, the big lie that multitudes swallow hook, line and sinker, is the illusion of affluence—not affluence itself but the illusion that affluence creates. It can be simply expressed by giving a positive twist to a negative statement of Jesus. He said that "a man's life does not consist in the abundance of his possessions" (Luke 12:15). The *illusion* says that a man's life does consist in the abundance of his possessions. According to its proponents the good life is essentially the prosperous life. An abundance of material things produces happiness; and the larger the abundance, the greater the happiness.

Many factors in modern life encourage this illusion. There is the historical factor about which J. K. Galbraith writes in his book, *The Affluent Society*.[1] He reminds us that throughout history the masses of people in all nations have been very poor; poverty was the all-pervasive fact of their life. In the last few generations, however, in Western Europe and in North America, even the common people have begun to enjoy an unprecedented affluence. There are political factors, notably the materialistic philosophy of Communism, also the socialist emphasis of the growing Welfare State which presses for a less unequal distribution of mankind's wealth. There are social factors such as advertising where "hidden persuaders" deliberately confuse our needs with our wants and try to convince us not only that certain luxuries are desirable but that only a dog can live without them. Most powerful of all is the psychological factor, the mood of sheer cupidity and covetousness which drives us to spend money we cannot afford to possess things we do not need in order to impress people we do not like.

Someone may react by saying, "This has nothing to do with me. I am a person of modest means. Indeed, I should like to cut myself in on a little of the affluence that everyone is

[1] Penguin Books, 1958.

talking about." Surely we do not have to be convinced that, in contrast with two-thirds of the human race, any person able to purchase and read this book belongs to an affluent society. We may have to be convinced that affluence is a state of mind. It consists in having enough of this world's goods, and "enough" is always just a bit more than we have now. A raise in salary, perhaps, or a mortgage-free house, or the means to take a holiday abroad—that's all we ask of life. Give us that, and we shall be happy. But therein lies the illusion of affluence. It is the sincere belief that enough material possessions can satisfy us and meet our deepest needs, a belief so utterly false that Jesus, though he spoke to comparatively poor people, lost no opportunity to puncture it.

Once a man came to him and burst out petulantly, "Teacher, bid my brother divide the inheritance with me." That was something more serious than the cry of a child, "Tell my brother to give me half of his apple!" Presumably the man felt defrauded of his share of inherited wealth and he hoped that Jesus would appeal to his brother's sense of fairness before he consulted a lawyer and took the case to court. Almost curtly Jesus replied, "Man, who made me a judge or a divider over you?" Something in the man's attitude bothered Jesus and compelled him to turn to the disciples and warn them, "Take heed, and beware of all covetousness; for a man's life does not consist in the abundance of his possessions." Then, to enforce his warning, he told them a parable about a small barn and a big fool which he followed with an unforgettable sermon about the providence of God—all of it a commentary on the one text, "A man's life does not consist in the abundance of his possessions."

Let us be very clear that Jesus did not despise material possessions. He taught that we shall best serve God not by renouncing our wealth but by accepting it gratefully as a gift from God and using it responsibly in a way of which God would approve. Though the teachings of Jesus arose out of a situation of material poverty, he saw no virtue in poverty, as some holy men have done. He saw poverty as one of the evils of society. His great compassionate heart went out to the poor people of his day, as it still goes out to the world's poor who are denied the food and clothing, shelter and security which most of us take for granted. Jesus would not deny that material things are necessary and that, wisely used, they are an ingredient of the good life. He would insist, however, that material things by themselves do not add up to life. Man, as God created him, is bigger than money, food, clothing, houses, motor-cars and gadgets. His life does not and cannot consist in the abundance of his possessions.

To explode the illusion of affluence we must re-state our Lord's Word positively and ask, In what *does* a man's life consist? Most of us would agree that it consists partly, at least, in *a feeling of inner contentment*. A very simple test proves the proposition. If a man's life did consist in the abundance of his possessions, the affluent people would be the happiest people, and the greater their affluence, the greater would be their happiness. Conversely, the poor people would be the miserable people, and the greater their poverty, the greater would be their misery. But does it always work out that way?

Returning from Scandinavia, a woman journalist found herself sitting in the aeroplane next to a young man who suddenly asked her, "Where would you like to live, you who have visited so many countries?" The question took her by surprise, and she could not return an immediate, clear-cut answer. Then she said, "Does it matter where you live so long as you are with the people you love and doing the work you like?" That did not satisfy the young man who went on to say that he meant such things as the beauty of the countryside, the standard of living, the welfare provided by the State, the extent of equality and hygiene, the affluence and what this affluence can buy.

It happened that the journalist had just been to Sweden, one of the most affluent countries in the world. Except for the climate, she said, Sweden has everything—money, education, beauty, taste, peace, full employment, welfare, motor boats, weekend cottages, supermarkets and shopping centres, the best design for living and excellent food. These ought to combine to make the Swedes the happiest people in the world; yet she had found them to be a discontented people, restless, bored with life and ridden with neuroses. It had occurred to her that the Southern Italians or the West Indians, who are still struggling for the bare necessities, derive more sheer joy out of life than do the affluent Swedes. "The happiest people I have met," she said, "are the aboriginals of Central Orissa, who go about singing and dancing clad in peacock feathers; the Nagas who are fighting not against India but against the destruction of their own happy-go-lucky way of life; and finally an old fisherman on the edge of a river in Haiti, who was singing as he mended his nets."[1]

It may be said also that a man's life consists in doing some kind of *work that gives him a sense of fulfilment*. Not long ago a group of people calling themselves "The Ad Hoc Committee on the Triple Revolution" presented the President of the United States with a staggering proposal. They suggested that every American should be guaranteed an adequate annual income whether or not he works. They listed three

[1] Taya Zinkmi, *The Guardian*, July 16, 1962.

current revolutions—human rights, weaponry and cybernation—and said that these change the economy so basically that very soon the old jobs-income pattern will no longer be viable in modern society. Right away we suspect that the committee consisted either of social parasites or of the writers of economic fiction. To our surprise we find among them a retired vice-president of the nation's largest insurance company, sociologists, scientists, economists, lawyers, political scientists, journalists and college professors—all of them competent, responsible and critical students of society, culture and economics. They were simply saying that, with machines and computers increasingly doing the work of men, the time is fast approaching when society will have to support its members and a man can say with truth that the world owes him a living.

We who were brought up on the old "work morality" will, of course, view this proposal not only as nonsense but as downright immoral. At once we ask, "What will happen to individual initiative and enterprise when we no longer earn our bread by the sweat of our brow? What incentive can we offer to our educators, scientists and artists if their work no longer yields a commensurate material reward?" The answer is these are the very people who may not need a material incentive, because their work is its own reward. After a television programme on which I had referred to Albert Einstein, one of the technicians asked me, "Is it true that Einstein was a wealthy man?" Another technician broke in, "What did Einstein need money for? He had his work." It was a shrewd comment. People who work primarily for material profit are usually those who do not enjoy their work but regard it as a grim necessity. Find a man with an interesting job, who feels that he is doing something useful, and if you tell him that his income will no longer be related to his productivity, he may grumble and even threaten to emigrate, but unless some labour union dictates otherwise, he will go on giving his best efforts, because his work yields its own sense of fulfilment. He enjoys his work for its own sake. His work is his life. Take that away from him, and no amount of material possessions can compensate for the loss.

Life consists *in our relationships with other people.* Indeed, so valuable are the benefits conferred by these relationships that no price tag can be placed on them. There is a significant verse in the 37th Psalm where the author says, "A little that a righteous man hath is better than the riches of many wicked." Comforting, but is it really true? Does it work out in terms of real life? Is a good man who makes £2,000 a year better off than a bad man who makes £200,000? The Psalmist comes close to the heart of the matter by repeatedly referring to a man's "seed", his children and grandchildren who are, after all, life's greatest treasure. Their love and loyalty become increasingly precious to a man, especially as he grows older. Without his children's affection all the money in the world is worthless. He knows from experience, however, that love, loyalty and respect do not come automatically from one's children. They are the rewards of goodness, the wealth of a righteous man, his source of happiness, even though he has little in the way of material possessions.

It means that the most precious commodities in life are not negotiable; they have nothing to do with material affluence. Love, trust, friendship, reputation—these make the poor man rich; without them the millionaire becomes a pauper. Shakespeare extols that theme in several of his plays. He makes Iago say,

"Who steals my purse steals trash; 'tis something, nothing;
'Twas mine, 'tis his, and has been slave to thousands;
But he who filches from me my good name,
Robs me of that which not enriches him.
And makes me poor indeed."

The same philosophy is echoed by the cruel Macbeth who, having murderously seized the throne of Scotland and all the wealth of royalty, found his nemesis, where many a person in later years finds it, in loneliness. After his wife's death, and with every man's hand against him, he awakened to the truth that a man's life does not consist in the abundance of his possessions:

"I have lived too long: my way of life
Is fall'n into the sear, the yellow leaf;
And that which should accompany old age,
As honour, love, obedience, troops of friends
I must not look to have."

Life consists in *the hope of eternity*. That is assuredly true, because the one thing of which we can be certain is that this life comes to an end. Our affluence may enable us to postpone the end for a few years but it does not change the essential situation. That was the point of the parable that Jesus told his disciples—the story of the farmer who had become so affluent that he decided to retire and said to his soul, "Soul, you have ample goods laid up for many years; take your ease, eat, drink and be merry." But God said to him, "Fool, this night your soul is required of you." Not that God proposed to kill him off. His time had run out, that's all, and where he was going he could not take his possessions with him. He planned to build bigger barns, but there are no bigger barns, not if you intend to store a human soul in them. If that's what you plan, then the barns become smaller and the foolishness grows larger until nothing is left but heaven's thunderous comment on the vast absurdity of it all, "Fool! This night your soul is required of you; and the things you have prepared, whose will they be?"

In her charming spiritual autobiography, *A Gift of Joy*,[1] Helen Hayes, the distinguished American actress, recalls a journey on the train with a beautiful woman whom she knew slightly. This woman was in the last stage of tuberculosis and was returning to her home in England to die. She had been a successful ballroom dancer with the usual string of admirers and had amassed a pretty collection of costly jewellery. She sent for Miss Hayes begging her to come to her private compartment. Conversation was impossible, since even the effort to whisper exhausted the sick woman, but it was not conversation that she wished. Very soon she indicated by a nod to her maid that she was ready for what was obviously a daily ritual. The maid placed a large leather jewel case before her, unlocked and opened it. For the next hour and a half Miss Hayes was required to take each piece from the drawers, hold it up to the light and turn it this way and that while the owner feverishly studied first the jewel then her face for a reaction. Miss Hayes says that her own exhibition of unalloyed delight was undoubtedly one of her finer performances as an actress. But she really wanted to cry. Here was a dying woman with nothing to show for her life, nothing to hang on to but a box of hard, bright objects which now amounted to no more than playthings. This was all that she had

[1] A Fawcett Crest Book, 1965.

left to help her through the final crisis. The illusion of affluence!

It all adds up to this—that a man's life consists in *his relationship to God.* Someone imagined God first fashioning man, and one of the Host of Heaven watching and exclaiming in alarm, "But you are giving this creature freedom; he will not be wise enough to handle it; he will boast in his own self-sufficiency. How can you gamble that he will ever return to you?" And God replies, "I have left him unfinished within. I have left in him deep needs that only I can satisfy; out of his desire, his homesickness of soul, he will remember and turn to me." The message of the Bible and the stern fact of human experience is that, if man does not remember to turn to God, if he tries to satisfy his spiritual hungers with material food, his soul, his inner self, his personal identity shrivels up and dies, and he discovers that he has lived through everything except life. Call it economic heresy, if you will, but life itself punctures the illusion of affluence and proves the truth of God's own Word spoken through his Son: "A man's life does not consist in the abundance of his possessions."

CHAPTER 2

THE ILLUSION OF SECURITY

"*For it would have been better for us to serve the Egyptians than to die in the wilderness.*" (Exodus 14:12.) Modern Israelis would not say that, but it was said by their ancestors, the ancient Israelites. I knew what they meant when I journeyed through the same wilderness a few years ago. It is the grimmest, most desolate, most forbidding stretch of land that I have ever seen—endless miles of barren desert waste, not a tree or a sign of vegetation anywhere. From dawn to dusk the parched sand reflects a scorching sun; and the traveller, unless he carries his own shade and water supply, will soon die of sunstroke or thirst. If any place on God's earth can be said to seem God-forsaken, it is this wilderness reaching from the Red Sea to the hills of Judea. Even today it remains uninhabited save for occasional Bedouins in their black goat-skin tents. How they survive or how any life could survive in that wilderness remains a mystery.

No wonder the Israelites became panicky. By the power of God a million of them had been delivered from slavery in Egypt and brought safely to the eastern shore of the Red Sea. They were free, but free for what—starvation, thirst, exposure? How could this desert ever sustain their life? Would it yield food and drink or would it become a vast graveyard that entombed their rotting bones long before they could ever reach the Promised Land? They looked over their shoulders at the Nile Valley yielding its lush harvests of grain and figs and pomegranates. True, they had been slaves in Egypt, but slaves with food to eat and water to drink. What fools they were to exchange even the limited security of slavery for a freedom that could only mean a slow, tortured death! Thereupon they began to murmur and they never stopped murmuring. Again and again, when danger stared them in the face and things did not go their way, they complained to Moses, their leader, "For it would have been better for us to serve the Egyptians than to die in the wilderness."

Not only do we understand the complaint but we can enter into the spirit of it and make it our own. Ever since the economic depression of the 1930's and World War Two, the peoples of the free world have been obsessed with making themselves secure. Security has become the god of the twentieth century upon whose altar men are prepared to pour out any sacrifice. Take a poll of the students in our universities and ask them the question, "What, as a result of your higher education, do you want most out of life?" Whereas a generation ago some might have replied that they want to make their mark in the world, now the majority will reply that they want security. Ask them to define the word, and they will speak in terms of the right to work, a guaranteed annual wage, unemployment benefits, pension schemes, the freedom to enjoy life knowing that they need not worry or be anxious about the future. We who are middle-aged have conditioned them to make exactly that response.

So the Old Testament speaks to our condition. "It would have been better for us to serve the Egyptians than to die in the wilderness." That is the complaint not of an ancient tribe but of man himself, man in this twentieth century, who gives absolute priority to his own security and who will pay almost any price to be secure. We need to look critically at this complaint, because it presupposes something that is simply not true. It was not true for the Israelites and it is not true for us. Security is an illusion which, in all fairness and honesty to ourselves, we need to puncture with the two-edged sword of Holy Scripture.

The Israelites had short memories, else they might have recalled with painful vividness that in Egypt they had been anything but secure. In his autobiography, Booker T. Washington, the American Negro educator, describes the reaction of the Negro slaves to the Emancipation Proclamation of 1863. First they gave themselves to rejoicing and thanksgiving and wild scenes of ecstasy, but as the responsibility and the hazards of being free gradually dawned upon them, little groups began trickling back to their slave quarters. The Negro slaves in America had known a certain measure of security, and some had been treated kindly. Not so the Hebrew slaves in Egypt. You have only to read the Bible to see that Moses had delivered them from a life of sheer hell, brutality, starvation and from the deadly whips of their cruel taskmasters.

They were not being realistic, otherwise they would have admitted that they could be secure neither in the wilderness nor in Egypt. On either terms any idea of security was an illusion. Here is the *first great lesson* that we can learn as we identify ourselves with the wandering Israelites. Security on any terms is an illusion. It is a lesson which many people have been taught by bitter experience.

> "We were to learn that man has no rights in his imagined security. In how few moments can its bulwarks be undermined! It seemed as if a tottering spire came crashing through our shuddering roof, walls meeting as they collapsed into the wreckage; everything smudged, smeared, senseless, silly chaos. 'I have to tell you,' the specialist said to me alone when the diagnosis was clear, 'that we have no cures.' He knew we wanted the whole truth. I left the hospital dazed."[1]

Those words tell their own story. They were written by a middle-aged man whose wife's sudden illness was diagnosed as progressive muscular atrophy. Two years later, after a heroic struggle, she died. It is the kind of disaster that could hit anyone and it shows with stark realism that in this world there are no earthly securities, no physical faculties, no material things, no human relationships, that cannot be snatched away from us. Until man devises some kind of life whereby his body shall be immune to illness and disease, his property invulnerable to fire and flood, and he himself exempt from the misfortunes and stupidities of his fellow-man—until then, security, as we understand it, will be an illusion.

The ancient Hebrews teach us a *second lesson*: it is possible to want to pay too high a price for security. For four hundred years they and their fathers had suffered in bondage. For four hundred years the succeeding generations had hoped and dreamed and prayed to be free. Now at last their prayers had been answered, and God's people for the first time in four centuries breathed the clean air of freedom.

[1] D. M. Wilson, *Triumph Over Fear*, Victor Gollancz Ltd., London, 1966.

Ahead of them lay the hardships, the perils, the insecurity of the wilderness, but also the challenge to meet and overcome those dangers and the opportunity to build themselves into the great independent nation promised to their forefathers. It was the crisis point, the finest hour in their history. Would they give it all up in return for a security that meant pig slops and forced labour and an existence where they could not call their souls their own?

People are doing exactly that in the world today, and some have lived to regret it. It will be a long time before another Hitler rises to power in Germany. To that proud nation, trampled into the dust of military defeat and humiliated by an unreasonable peace treaty, Hitler appeared as a political Messiah, offering the German people a new prosperity, a new purpose, a new place under the sun. They accepted his offer but they gave their souls in exchange for it. A totalitarian State, sustained by its preparations for war, combed with concentration camps and terrorized by the Gestapo—such was the price that Germany paid for security in the 1930's. It will not readily pay that price again.

The illusion of security has a humorous side. It recalls the conversation between Alice and the White Knight in *Through the Looking Glass*:

"'But you've got a beehive or something like it fastened to the saddle,' said Alice.

"'Yes, it's a very good beehive,' the knight said in a discontented tone, 'one of the best kind. But not a single bee has come near it yet. And the other thing is a mouse trap. I suppose the mice keep the bees out, or the bees keep the mice out, I don't know which.'

"'I was wondering what the mouse trap is for,' said Alice.

'It isn't very likely there would be any mice on the horse's back.'

"'Not very likely, perhaps,' said the knight, 'but if they do come, I don't choose to have them running all about. You see,' he went on after a pause, 'it's as well to be provided for *everything*.'"

We can pay too high a price for security, such a price that we appear as ridiculous as the addle-pated White Knight on his overloaded horse. The illusion of security drives people to do some very foolish things—to sacrifice their freedom, their initiative, their opportunities, their ideals, all that makes life worth living. When Sir Oliver Franks was British Ambassador in Washington he warned us to be on our guard against establishing a society which mistakes comfort for civilization. As nations and as individuals we may save our lives only to lose them, forgetting that strength of character, national and personal, is forged only in the furnace of discipline, adventure and hard work. You cannot have courage without adventure, sympathy without suffering, tenderness without weakness or pain. You can't have your own soul and total security as well. That is what the Spanish mystic, Unamuno, meant when he concluded his book, *The Tragic Sense of Life*, with the prayer, "May God deny you peace but give you glory."

For God's people it was an illusion to suppose that Egypt held greater security than the wilderness because it assumed that security is the chief end of life, and we know that there are some values in life more precious than security. That is the *third lesson* we learn by looking at the Israelites. In our modern idiom they were saying something like "better red than dead". They were taking the popular line that nothing matters except staying alive and that life must be preserved at any cost, even the sacrifice of ideals and values for which past generations have struggled and suffered and paid the price of blood. If that were the right line to take, we should not be facing such a choice today, because the human race would have committed moral suicide a long time ago. Israel survived only because Moses persisted in taking the opposite and unpopular line—that it was better, in fact, to die in the wilderness than to serve the Egyptians. Moses had lived behind the Egyptian "iron curtain", so he knew what he was talking about.

We can imagine that Moses laughed at his people. "Better the security of slavery than the hazards of freedom," they said. But what did they know about freedom or security, they who had been worked like machines and driven like beasts in the stone quarries and brickyards? It was he, Moses, who had been free and secure, first as a prince of Egypt, then as a prosperous farmer in Midian. But Moses caught a vision of something grander and worthier than personal security, a vision of the will and purpose of God. Centuries later a Christian writer could inscribe this epitaph on his tomb: "By faith Moses, when he was come to years, refused to be called the son of Pharaoh's daughter, choosing rather to suffer affliction with the children of God than to enjoy the pleasures of sin for a season." (Hebrews 11:24, 25.)

Louis Evans tells of visiting a mission hospital in Korea and spending some time with the missionary doctor, a man who in answer to the call of God gave up a lucrative practice in America. One day the doctor said, "Would you like to see a major operation?" Evans replied that he would. Minutes later he was standing in the operating-room balcony along with a number of Korean medical students. The operation took seven hours. Several times he found the intense heat and ether fumes so overbearing that he had to go outside to refresh himself. When it was all over, he asked, "Doctor, is every day like this?" The surgeon only smiled. Beads of perspiration stood on his brow, his lips were purple with the strain, his hands trembled with fatigue. "Doctor," asked Evans, "how much would you be paid for an operation like this back in America?" "About five hundred dollars," came the reply. "It was a complicated case." "How much will you get for it here?" The doctor turned and looked at the poor Korean woman who had been wheeled into the operating room clutching only a copper coin and begging him to save her life. With tears welling up in his fine eyes, he said, "For this I will get her gratitude and my Master's smile." Then he added, "But that, sir, is worth more to me than all the money that the world can give."[1]

The story of the Christian Faith is a story of contempt for security as we understand it: the story of Peter and John, threatened with imprisonment but retorting, "We ought to obey God rather than men!" It is the story of Paul pursuing his perilous missionary journeys over land and sea, persecuted by his enemies and betrayed by his friends; the story of martyrs yielding their bodies to the mouths of lions; of Reformers sacrificing, as Luther said, "goods, honour, children, wife"; of missionaries leaving home to face the rigours and loneliness of life in foreign lands; of churches under the iron cross of tyranny where men choose to die for God rather than live for Satan. These are the great souls of the race, the saviours of mankind, men and women who

[1] Louis H. Evans, *Youth Seeks A Master*, New York, Fleming H. Revell Company, 1951, pp. 80–81.

believed and lived out their belief that there are values in life more precious than their own security.

The Israelites did not die in the wilderness. In obeying God they found their only real security. That is the *greatest lesson* which they teach us. From the moment they responded to God's initiative and took the venture of faith they were guided and sustained by the protecting power of God. When they came to the forbidding obstacle of the Red Sea, a strong east wind drove back the waters, enabling them to cross as on dry land. When hunger gnawed at their stomachs, manna fell from heaven, and a passing flock of quails furnished fresh meat. When thirst drove them wild, Moses struck a porous rock and brought forth a gush of clear, cool water. When hostile tribes attacked them, superhuman powers drove the Israelites to victory. When inner strife threatened to demoralize them, they were given laws so enduring that they have become the basis of our civilization. God did not guarantee security to his people as they hesitated on the edge of that grim, barren wilderness, but as long as they moved forward in trustful and obedient faith they found in God an unfailing source of security.

This is the unfailing promise of the Bible. Scripture throbs with assurance of the Providence of God. It tells us that the very hairs of our head are numbered. It tells us that God, who feeds the birds of the air and dresses the flowers of the field, will certainly provide for his human creatures as he sees their needs. It tells us that nowhere in this universe can we pass beyond the care of the Almighty Father. Even death cannot separate us from his love. It tells us that in the most unnerving crisis we may ever come to know we can be upheld by the confidence that the last word in life and the world is not hunger, poverty, cancer, insanity, war or death but a Divine love and power working for our good, and certain to triumph in the end.

Security is an illusion because security is a state of mind. All the money, property, investments and insurance policies in the world will never make a man secure as long as he has a definite supply of insecurity stored up inside him. If there is any security at all, we must look for it in ourselves. We must look for it not in the material things that can be taken away from us but in the relationship of our lives to the great securities which stand like mountains majestic and serene in the midst of all upheaval and change. To be secure your life must be related to something secure, something that will outlast it and give it meaning and worth. Security depends not on the direction of the stock market but on the direction of your ultimate loyalties. Martin Niemoller said that he felt secure even in a concentration camp. He declared, "Not Hitler but God is my Führer"; and in loyalty to eternal Truth and Right he found an inner peace passing understanding.

Inevitably we come into the presence of the most secure man who ever lived. Jesus began his adult life in a carpenter's shop where he was comfortable and reasonably secure. But God asked him, "Are you ready?" and Jesus answered "Yes". The crowds deserted him, and the Pharisees growled, "This innovator must be stopped!" So they hounded and hunted him to a cross. God said, "Can you bear it for my sake and theirs?" Jesus replied, "Yes". So they nailed him to a Cross and left him to die there, forsaken and defeated. But all the way from the carpenter's shop to the Cross Jesus remained the securest man who ever lived, talking about peace when his situation was not peaceful, about joy when the circumstances around were not joyous. His was the security of life in God, the security of surrender to God, the only permanent security that there is. He promises to give us that security as we identify ourselves with him and surrender our lives to God in trust and obedience.

CHAPTER 3

THE ILLUSION OF NEUTRALITY

Of all the illusions nursed by modern man none is more pathetic or dangerous than the illusion of neutrality. It is the mistaken idea that one can detach oneself from any kind of conflict and watch as a spectator from the sidelines. Political neutrality sits squarely on the back of neither horse that pulls the wagon of the body politic but attempts the ridiculous posture of riding two or three horses at the same time. Social neutrality straddles the fence of public opinion and refuses to come down on either side in the great social issues. Moral neutrality shows itself in a broadminded tolerance which sees good and evil not in terms of black and white but in terms of differing shades of grey. Spiritual neutrality chooses neither belief nor atheism but leaves the matter open by walking the middle road of agnosticism.

Here is a man who maintains the posture of neutrality. He works as a minor clerk in somebody's firm and lives quietly with his family in a modest suburban home. "I am a peaceful man," he is fond of saying. He has no enemies simply because he has no strong opinions. He rarely involves himself in an argument; and when discussions do arise at home or at the office or among his circle of friends, he never takes sides. He has the reputation for being able to see both points of view.

Nobody knows where he stands politically, how he votes or whether he votes at all. Even his children cannot draw him out to settle their disputes or shape their attitudes towards the problems that face the younger generation. He goes to church but not militantly, because some of his colleagues and friends have no use for the Church. If issues threaten to divide the congregation, he keeps his feet firmly planted in both camps. This man is a moral acrobat. In all of life's relationships he has mastered the difficult trick of straddling the fence and he compliments himself on cleverly preserving the posture of neutrality.

In her book, *Creed or Chaos*, Dorothy Sayers calls neutrality a sin. She equates it with the Sixth Deadly Sin to which the Medieval Church gave the old-fashioned name of "Sloth". "It is the sin which believes in nothing, cares for nothing, seeks to know nothing, interferes with nothing, enjoys nothing, loves nothing, hates nothing, finds purpose in nothing, lives for nothing, and only remains alive because there is nothing it would die for." About neutrality she adds, "We have known it too well for many years. The only thing perhaps that we have not known about it is that it is a mortal sin."

Strong language, to be sure, but it makes sense, especially when we couple it with the words of Edmund Burke, "All that is needed for the triumph of evil is that good men do nothing". In actual fact there is no such thing as neutrality. It is an illusion, a form of self-deception that exists only in the mind of the self-deceiver. No man can remain neutral in the things that really matter, and that becomes obvious in the light of certain persuasive considerations.

Consider, first, that *neutrality is a luxury for which somebody has to pay the price.* About ten years ago, at a conference in Washington, I listened to a stirring address by a United States senator. By that time the Korean War had dramatized the ambitions of Communism and had stabbed us broad awake to the realities of the world power struggle. The senator was talking about the nations that stood aloof from the struggle and refused to align themselves with East or West. Their attitude of moral superiority got under his skin. "These nations," he said, "can afford to be neutral only because other countries, by maintaining the balance of power, make it possible for them to be neutral. They know that the West will defend them. Let the West withhold its protection, and they will not be able to remain neutral for very long."

In terms of practical politics the senator may or may not have been right. In principle he expounded a very important truth. Somebody has to pay the price of another's neutrality. Nations and individuals can stand apart from a struggle only as long as other nations and other individuals are fighting that struggle for them. Let everybody try to maintain the posture of neutrality, and sooner or later the struggle will be lost by default.

A hundred years ago the Negro slaves in the United States were declared free. Their freedom came at terrific cost, not only because some Americans favoured slavery but also because the great majority of Americans held no strong convictions one way or the other. Men in high places tried to maintain a discreet posture of neutrality. They did not realize that their continued equivocation might ultimately destroy the Union. What saved the Union was the unequivocal partisanship of men like Abraham Lincoln who struck out fearlessly on this crucial issue of human rights. Even as a young man Lincoln had taken a stand. In New Orleans where he saw Negroes chained and whipped at the slave auction he exclaimed to his friends, "By God, boys, let's get away from this. If ever I get a chance to hit this thing, I'll hit it hard." He did hit it hard. Speaking years later in New York during his Presidential campaign, he asked, "What do you think will content the South?" "Nothing," he answered, "but the acknowledgement that slavery is morally right and socially elevating." This being so, he said, there was no use in "groping about for some middle ground between right and wrong" or in "a policy of 'don't care' on a question about which all true men do care".

The symbol of neutrality in our culture is the "hippie" (or "beatnik" or "yippie"; the terms may be interchangeable). Perhaps we do not understand the psychology, still less the jargon of these young men and women who colonize in slums and assume the appearance of human freaks. Social scientists tell us that they are not evil, though it might be better for them if they were evil, because it would bring them into closer touch with reality. The "hippie" is neutral towards good and evil. He wants to be left alone to make love and smoke "pot". As a form of passive protest against the problems of a "square" world he simply opts out of it. He would have much more to protest against if it were not for high-minded young people with a sense of social responsibility who prepare themselves to deal positively, actively and constructively with the problems of the square world from which he has opted out. They pay the price of his neutrality.

Neutrality is always a luxury for which somebody has to pay the price. That is true in relation to the Church. Despite a growing general indifference, the majority of people in our society today are not opposed to the Church and what it stands for. They are neither for the Church nor against it.

They would describe themselves as neutral. Of course, if everybody assumed that posture, there would soon be no Church either to support or oppose. The Church, as we know it, would pass out of existence, and with it would go the mainspring of Christianity, the one institution that keeps alive the ethic and redemptive power of God's revelation in Christ. People who remain neutral to the Church have no imagination. They need to visualize our society as it would fast become if the churches had to close their doors; and the churches would close their doors but for the faithful few who pay the price to keep them open. Some people can afford to be neither for nor against the Church only because others continue to be stubbornly and devotedly for it.

Consider also that neutrality is an illusion, because *the refusal to choose does itself constitute a choice.* Concerning religion a man will say, "I shall not become a Christian, because there are too many obstacles in the path of belief, too many questions that have not been answered to my private satisfaction. I am not an atheist. I do not deny the existence of God. But neither am I convinced that God does exist or, if he exists, that Christianity is the right religion. Therefore I shall withhold my judgment and continue to look at the matter impartially." We respect this man's honesty and we shall not attempt to force him to a decision. Obviously he must make up his own mind. Let him understand, however, that time does not stand still while he weighs the pros and cons of religious truth. The stream moves forward. He may refuse to make up his mind but he cannot refuse to make up his life. That gets made up one way or the other.

The same thing is true on a social scale. For many years I lived in a community where people observed the Christian

Sabbath and where Sabbath observance was protected by law. From time to time big business interests agitated for a change in the laws and brought the issue to a popular vote. Eventually by a small majority the city voted in favour of commercialized Sunday sport. The Christian conscience was shocked, not only because it happened but because it need not have happened. What tipped the scales was not the number of people who went to the polls and voted "Yes" in the plebiscite—they had a democratic right to do so—but the larger number of people who, unable to make up their minds and unwilling to take a stand, stayed at home and did not vote "Yes" or "No". They found that their refusal to choose did itself constitute a choice.

Whatever we may think of Communism, at least the Marxists do not make a virtue of neutrality. Speaking at the United Nations General Assembly in October, 1961, the Nationalist Chinese Foreign Minister quoted from the Peking *New Terminology Dictionary* which defines the term "Neutralist Line" as follows: "A day-dream that can never be realized. Even in theory it is not correct. As the world situation stands today there are only two roads—either to support capitalism or to support socialism—and there is no third road. Any vain hope to take a third road is doomed to failure." Could any statement be clearer? It should be compulsory reading for politicians and labour leaders and social reformers and youthful idealists who nurse a romantic illusion about the possibility of our being uncommitted anywhere in the world. We do not hear the Marxists talking about being uncommitted. They are precisely committed, and so are all men and all nations if they face the truth honestly.

Two choices do confront men today but they are more

basic and more crucial than the choice between opposing political theories. They touch the deepest issues of human life, the ultimate questions that have to be answered one way or the other: Does life make sense or is it simply nonsense? Is life a meaningless struggle or is it nurtured in the purpose and goodness of Almighty God? Are we insects with no more significance than a fly on a window-pane or are we the children of a wise and loving Father? Are the love and kindness and generosity which we show in our finest hours indications of the true nature of life or are they just so much sentimental weakness? What is more important—people or things, individuals or institutions? Do governments exist to be served or do they exist to serve? Is God or is he not? Was Jesus a dreamer and a psychopathic fool or did he know how life at its best should be lived? Two choices—God's way or the God-denying way. Life forces them upon us. Whatever we believe with our minds, our lives are committed to one or the other. There can be no middle ground, no neutrality.

Turning to the Word of God, we find in Scripture a recurring theme that punctures the illusion of neutrality. It is that: *God does not recognize neutrals.* When he holds before us the great moral and spiritual choices that touch our lives and the life of our society he insists that we take a stand and come down firmly on one side or the other.

There is a dramatic scene described in the closing chapter of the Old Testament Book of Joshua. After four hundred years of slavery in Egypt and forty years of wandering in the wilderness, during which they have been welded into a great, united nation, the children of Israel have entered the Promised Land. God has brought this miracle to pass, God who raised up Moses to lead Israel out of bondage, God who divided the waters of the Red Sea, who guided his people by pillars of cloud and fire, fed them with manna from heaven, gave them eternal laws, brought them across the Jordan River, destroyed the walls of Jericho and made the very elements fight against Israel's enemies. It seems unthinkable that Israel should ever be tempted now to forget her God, much less be attracted by the impotent gods of her pagan neighbours. Yet Joshua saw the need to warn his nation against this peril. On a memorable day he assembled all the people at Shechem and showed them in words a motion picture of the events of their history from the call of Abraham through the centuries to their own day. In the light of God's dealings with them in history let them once and for all decide: "Now, therefore, fear the Lord, and serve him in sincerity and faithfulness; put away the gods which your fathers served beyond the river, and in Egypt, and serve the Lord. And if you be unwilling to serve the Lord, choose this day whom you will serve . . . As for me and my house, we will serve the Lord." (Joshua 24:14, 15.)

No less dramatic is a scene described in the Book of First Kings. It is set against the towering background of Mount Carmel. At the foot of the mountain are two altars laden with faggots and the sacrificial bulls. Surrounding one of them are 750 prophets of the gods of Baal and Ashera. To one side stand the weak King Ahab and Jezebel, his wicked queen; and behind them, filling the whole picture and reaching out of sight, are the hosts of the children of Israel. Near the second altar stands a solitary figure, the prophet Elijah, called by Ahab, the "troubler of Israel". Elijah will presently match the strength of his God against the weakness of the false gods, but not to impress royalty whom he despises or the pagan priests for whom he has only contempt. Let the wicked stand where they will. Elijah's concern is for the common people who have not the courage to take a stand one way or another. Ignoring his enemies, he shouts to the uncommitted masses, "How long will you go limping with two different opinions? If the Lord is God, follow him, but if Baal, then follow him." (I Kings 18:21.)

We express our disgust for a thing by saying, "It makes me sick!" Difficult, perhaps, to believe that the God who went to the uttermost limits of love on the Cross of Calvary could ever react with such nausea; yet according to the New Testament Book of Revelation the one thing that does make God sick is neutrality. The Church at Laodicea presents us for the first time in history with the picture of a large, successful, affluent congregation. We see a Christian community which has succumbed to all the perils of prosperity—smugness, complacency, self-sufficiency and inertia. It was really not a church at all but a religious club to which the best people felt that they owed it to themselves to belong. Their passionless religion amounted to nothing more than a respectable morality. Piety they deplored, enthusiasm they considered vulgar; and on the great moral issues of their day they were neither cold nor hot but sickeningly tepid. Therefore they made God sick. "So because you are lukewarm," he said, "and neither cold nor hot, I will spew you out of my mouth." (Revelation 3:16.)

One of Britain's great preachers, the late W. E. Sangster, went with his son to a cricket match between Surrey and Sussex. Before the start of the game Dr. Sangster tapped his son on the knee and said, "Now, my boy, let's have none of your nonsense about 'May the best team win'. I don't want the best team to win. I want Surrey to win. Is that clear?" It was clear to the young man who lovingly wrote his father's biography and it was typical of his father's outlook. Dr. Sangster was vehemently partisan not only towards sport but towards the more serious issues. He saw all of life as a crucial conflict between the Kingdom of Christ and the Kingdom of Satan and he wanted Christ to win. He never nursed the illusion of neutrality.

No Christian nurses the illusion of neutrality. He cannot be neutral when he follows the most un-neutral Man who ever lived. Jesus of Nazareth lived on this earth a life of perfect obedience to God, a life so completely committed to God's way for men that inevitably it brought him into conflict with those who were opposed to that way. It is the life that God intends us to live; and unless we are prepared to live it, prepared even to suffer for our commitment to God, then we identify ourselves not with Christ but with those who nailed him to a Cross. That is what Jesus meant when he punctured the illusion of neutrality by saying, "He that is not for me is against me."

CHAPTER 4

THE ILLUSION OF INDEPENDENCE

When the Commonwealth Prime Ministers' Conference met in London, a daily newspaper published a list of representative countries, and beside each country the date on which it became independent. I couldn't help asking, "Independent of what?" Of colonial rule, perhaps, but certainly not of colonial friendship. The very nations which today most vehemently agitate for self-rule are the nations least able to stand on their own feet. Even when they fly their distinctive flags they still have to depend for economic aid and technical assistance upon countries older and stronger than themselves. They soon discover that, except as a political theory, independence is an illusion. In the complex relationships of our modern world even the richest and most powerful nations cannot claim complete independence.

Neither can the individual claim to be independent. Occasionally you hear someone make the empty boast, "I am a self-made man." Cynicism tempts us to tell such a person, "Sir, you have just relieved God of a solemn responsibility." In kindness we remind him that a self-made man is a biological impossibility. Each of us owes his existence to the male and female who co-operated in the act of his creation. We all owe our survival to parents or foster-parents who protected and cared for us during the helplessness of our infancy and childhood. We owe our bodily skills and our mental equipment to the knowledge accumulated by past generations and the teachers who instructed us in that knowledge. We owe our present opportunities, however limited, to the society in which we live, to governments, employers, doctors, farmers, policemen and other men and women who pursue their vocations as faithfully as we pursue ours. Albert Einstein once said, "Many times a day I realize how much my own inner and outer life is built upon the labours of my fellow-men, both living and dead, and how earnestly I must exert myself in order to give in return as much as I have received." The greatest men have known that in the midst of life we are in debt. They have not nursed the illusion of independence.

Yet one illusion that persists stubbornly in our culture is the idea that we can be independent of God. It is not new but it is certainly being preached with a new religious zeal. One of its great high priests, Sir Julian Huxley, in his book, *The Humanist Frame*,[1] writes of an "evolutionary religion" which will help man to achieve his full stature in a godless universe. Huxley believes that man must learn to face the problems of his environment with no outside help. Writes Huxley, "Evolutionary man can no longer take refuge from his loneliness by creeping for shelter into the arms of a divinized father figure whom he has himself created, nor escape from the responsibility of making decisions by sheltering under the umbrella of Divine Authority, nor absolve himself from the hard task of meeting his present problems and planning his future by relying on the will of an omniscient but unfortunately inscrutable Providence."

[1] Allen and Unwin, 1961.

That kind of talk pleases a lot of people. It is the "conventional wisdom" which they can understand, with which they can agree and which builds up their self-esteem. But is it true? Flattering as the illusion of independence may be to modern man's vanity, it cannot be reconciled with the truths embodied in the great doctrines of the Christian Faith. The doctrine of *Creation* proclaims the truth that the world in which we live did not begin with a "big bang", as some astronomers claim, but with a purposeful creative act of God. The doctrine of *Providence* proclaims the truth that God watches over his creation experiment, cares for his creatures, provides for their needs, involves himself in their life and governs the world according to his wise and loving purpose. The doctrine of *Redemption* proclaims the truth that, when proud man entertains illusions of independence and rebels against God's purpose, God does not leave man to destroy himself but comes where man is and rescues him from his predicament.

At least one class of people did not nurse the illusion of independence. They were the poets of Israel who poured out their praise to God in the Psalms. "O Lord, how manifold are thy works! In wisdom hast thou made them all: the earth is full of thy riches." (Psalm 104:24.) The Psalmist cannot contain his wonder as he surveys the marvellous design of God's creation. Here is the earth stocked like a giant storehouse with abundant supplies of water, vegetables and minerals; here are the oceans teeming with fish and resources yet untapped. Even the cattle on their pastures and the birds of the air and the wild animals of the wilderness live by the generosity of their Creator. Here are the seasons of summer and winter, the sunshine and rain that make possible the regularity of seedtime and harvest. Here are the day and night ordering man's life according to a rhythm of work and rest and giving him the strength and opportunity to draw from nature's storehouse and subdue the earth to his needs. The 104th Psalm is an anthem of praise to God for his mighty works in Creation: "O Lord, how manifold are thy works! In wisdom hast thou made them all: the earth is full of thy riches."

To be sure, the Hebrew poet lived in a pre-scientific age, but there is nothing unscientific about his insights. The most modern scientist, if he were a man of faith, would not argue with the Psalm. He would bring it up to date and employ modern thought-forms to express the wisdom and power of God. The astronomer might tell us about the uniqueness of the planet earth in our solar system, of how the earth is so tilted on its axis to revolve around its axis and so related to the sun as to follow a steady path around the sun, providing for alternate night and day, heat and cold, thereby making life on its surface possible. The geologist might take us down to the heart of the earth, bringing us up step by step through the geological ages and showing us the abundant resources of gold, iron, coal, oil and uranium which were stored there long before the arrival of man, and which provide the basic materials of our civilization. The botanist might fascinate us with a picture of nature's beauty in the chemistry of a wild flower, and the physiologist might point to the intricate mechanism of the human body. It is not surprising that some of the great scientists, in their study of nature which Robert Boyle called "God's Other Bible", have classed themselves among the ranks of devoutly religious men. They have not nursed the illusion of independence.

Someone has said that, though Henry Ford and his family

own the Ford Motor Company, yet if Mr. Ford set out by himself to build one Ford car he would soon discover his dependence on natural resources all over the earth and within the earth which he did not create and does not have the power to create. That is true of man himself as he flies to the moon or splits the atom or bakes bread or plucks the flowers in his garden. Man discovers truth but he does not create it. Man probes the secrets of nature, but they are still the secrets of nature. Man works the works of God, but they are still the works of God. Man manipulates the scheme of things but he does not add anything to the scheme of things. Man makes new combinations and arrangements but he does it within the order of God's Creation. Man can no more be independent of God the Creator than a child, growing up in his father's house, can be independent of his father.

A few years ago I accompanied a party of pilgrims who were being conducted through the Ein Gev Kibbutz on the eastern shore of the Sea of Galilee. Our guide, who boasted the Biblical name of Moses Ezekiel, pointed proudly to the miracles which the Jews have worked with that barren country since they reclaimed it in 1948. Here were rows of tidy houses looking as attractive as a modern motel. Here were vineyards and groves of banana trees that yielded an abundant harvest for export. Here were date palms from which one could pluck the most succulent fruit ever to touch the lips. Here were barns housing pure-bred cattle. Here was a huge auditorium to which the great symphony orchestras of the world came to give concerts. One found all the amenities of life, all the signs of civilization with one notable exception. There was no synagogue, no house of worship—a startling omission among people of spiritual genius who have bequeathed to the world its religious heritage. Questioned about it, Moses Ezekiel laughed and said, "Why build a synagogue when nobody wants to pray? Better to spend the money on something useful like a tractor."

It was a case of history repeating itself. Three thousand years ago God delivered Israel from tyranny, just as he delivered these modern Israeli Jews from the ghettos of the world; and he brought his covenant people back to the Promised Land after they had been exiled from it for centuries. Moses, their leader, knew how quickly they might forget in their prosperity the God to whom they had prayed so fervently from the depths of suffering. He knew that they might begin to imagine themselves independent of God and to nurse the illusion that their own ingenuity and strength had brought this miracle to pass. They might even turn away from God and worship idols of their own devising, the work of their own hands, the ancient counterpart of tractors. This could only be their undoing, the disintegration of their common life and the shattering of their new nationhood. Therefore, as the people of Israel stood on the threshold of the Promised Land, Moses brought them together in solemn convocation and spoke to them for several hours. After reminding them of all that they owed to God and of the rich promise that God held in store for them, he gave stern warning: "Beware lest you say in your heart, 'My power and the might of my hand have gotten me this wealth' . . . If you forget the Lord your God . . . I solemnly warn you this day that you shall surely perish." (Deuteronomy 8: 17, 19.)

That is God's unchanging Word to an affluent society. In Archibald MacLeish's play *J.B.*, which is a modern adaptation of the Bible story of Job, the Devil says, "Piety's hard enough to take among the poor who have to practise it. A rich man's piety stinks." Something usually denudes the rich man of his piety; something insulates him against God.

That sort of thing is happening in our society today. We are rich beyond the wildest imaginings of our forefathers. We have developed a civilization with comforts, amenities and privileges of which past generations could not even have dreamed. We have learned to control diseases that once decimated whole populations. We have harnessed the very laws of nature for our own comfort and well-being. And our affluence is making us godless. We have begun to feel like gods ourselves, independent of the Creator and Ruler of the universe whose Providence alone makes our prosperity possible. Therefore, across the centuries comes the warning which, if we heed it seriously, will puncture the illusion of independence: "Beware lest you say in your heart, 'My power and the might of my hand have gotten me this wealth' . . . If you forget the Lord your God . . . I solemnly warn you this day that you shall surely perish."

A character in a modern novel says to an old lady who begs him to pray to Jesus for help, "I don't need no help from Jesus. I am doing all right by myself." *Here* is the illusion of independence—the supposition that man is doing all right by himself. Man has come of age. He has learned to master his material world and control his physical environment. Given a little time, he will find the answer to his basically human problems. "I don't need no help from Jesus. I'm doing all right by myself." Astonishing, surely, that the outlets of our culture—the universities, the libraries, the newspapers and the theatre—should still nurse this illusion, astonishing after the *dis*-illusioning events of modern history.

In a recent book, Bishop Lesslie Newbegin recalls conversing with a man who was a member of the team of physicists that worked on the first atomic bomb in Chicago during the final years of World War Two. This man described the sudden change of feeling which came over him and his colleagues when they sensed their success and realized that the thing they had created was potentially the most monstrous evil ever set loose in the world. Because the nature of their work imposed absolute secrecy, they could not share their sense of anxiety and guilt with anyone outside; they had to work out the moral problem for themselves. The scientist told Bishop Newbegin how he and the others formed a series of groups to study every aspect of their problem—historical, ethical, religious, legal; how they bought and devoured books on subjects they had never studied before; how they finally wrote to President Truman urging that the bombs should be used only in some uninhabited area after due warning and not in any case on a city; how their letter was never even answered; and how they had to see the instrument they had created used to create the horrors of Hiroshima and Nagasaki. These scientists found that at the moment of their apparent triumph they were simply tools for an operation against which their moral sense revolted. Bishop Newbegin comments:

> "A good deal has been written at present about man's coming of age. Much of the traditional language of Biblical religion is written off as belonging to a period when man felt himself unequal to the task of mastering his environment and when he had perforce to invoke the aid of alleged supernatural powers. Today, by contrast, it is suggested that man has grown out of this childish mentality. Today he knows how to control the powers of his environment . . . But this is only half the truth . . . Alongside of, or perhaps

underneath, the sense of mastery, the assurance that we are only at the beginning of the development made possible by modern techniques, there is also a sense of something like meaninglessness and even terror as man faces his future."[1]

Whoever nurses the illusion of independence has not looked objectively at our human situation. Suppose we try to do exactly that. Suppose we could project ourselves far enough into time or space to permit a coldly detached and scientific study of man's life on this earth over a period of a few thousand years, by what factor would we be most impressed? Surely by the futility of man's great and fantastic efforts to help himself. We should see a creature who, while he makes marvellous progress, is himself not progressive. Through all the revolutions wrought by his inventive genius he remains basically the same, living in this nuclear age as irrationally as he did in the dark ages—to his own and his neighbour's detriment. We should see a creature so at the mercy of temporary ignorance, mass social forces and his own endocrine glands that he is primarily the *victim* of evil rather than the doer of it. We should see him caught up in a spiral of inexorable circumstance, doing what he does not want to do, making decisions that he does not want to make and letting loose upon himself evil powers that betray his plans and curse his hopes. And we should be moved to exclaim, "This creature needs help! He needs a Saviour who will enter his situation from the outside and rescue him from this awful mess."

The Christian doctrine of Redemption proclaims the truth that there *is* a Saviour who does enter our situation from the outside to rescue us and whom we reject at our own peril.

[1] Lesslie Newbegin, *Honest Religion for Secular Man*, S.C.M. Press, London, 1966.

The story is told of how the French General Gallieni, once military Governor of Lyons, had offered a way out for the salvation of Paris. He planned to strike the right flank of the German army by using the vehicles of Paris to transport his troops to the front. But first he had to obtain permission from General Foch. For reasons of security he came to his superior's camp disguised in an old-fashioned, worn-out French uniform. He looked so nondescript in this ridiculous outfit that a junior officer, not waiting for an explanation, ordered him out of the camp. Later the officer told General Foch of the visitor and said that his name was Gallieni. Foch exploded, as only an army top brass can explode, when he heard of this undiplomatic treatment of a great General. The aide protested, "But who would take seriously an old man dressed up like that?" "That man", retorted Foch, "had a plan that could save the city of Paris and the lives of a million men."

It is a figure of the Christian Gospel. There comes into our besieged world a Galilean with a plan that would save any city and far more than a million men. He comes in the outmoded garb of the first century but he is the same yesterday, today and for ever. He comes from God. He brings us not only the answer but the power to resolve our human predicaments. He, the Christ of God, is the world's Saviour. If we believe in him, we shall not perish but have eternal life.

CHAPTER 5

THE ILLUSION OF MATURITY

Closely allied to the illusion of independence is the illusion of maturity. It is by no means modern but is as old as man himself. It was the illusion entertained by Adam and Eve in the Garden of Eden and was thrust on them by the serpent who proved to be a genuine "snake in the grass". People who get side-tracked into heated debates about the historical and scientific accuracy of the third chapter of Genesis miss the truth of the story altogether. They forget that the Bible is not nor does it claim to be a text-book on geology. Made up of sermons, poetry, biography and historical narrative, the Bible is an interpretation, from a particular point of view, of human existence. Since the dawn of his consciousness man has asked certain basic questions concerning the origin of his world, the source of his own life, the problem of good and evil, the mystery of what lies beyond. The Bible presents us with one attempt, a theological attempt, to answer those questions.

No question comes closer to home than that which concerns the dreadful predicament in which modern man has landed himself. So phenomenal has been his conquest of the universe, so remarkable the harnessing of nature's energy and resources, that his world should be a paradise, overflowing, as it does, with every condition for stability and happiness. Instead, we confront a chaos, an age of terror, of global disintegration and misery unknown to any previous generation. According to a United Nations research team, the great world powers now possess enough nuclear warheads to destroy our civilization and to eliminate all mankind. A sea of blazing rubble; no water, gas, electricity or sewers; 360,000 dead and 90,000 injured; people wandering about the streets in a state of shock; contaminated food; insanity; increase in cancerous diseases, especially leukaemia—such would be the effects of a single small bomb dropped on a city of one million people. Here is the paradox of our time—that in order to survive on this planet we have to depend for protection on caged monsters, knowing that if ever we unleash these monsters, they will turn on us and devour us.

What has gone wrong? How shall we diagnose our predicament? With that burning question the Bible in its opening chapters comes to grips. Scripture tells us that the world did indeed begin as a paradise and so it would have remained, had man, the tenant, been content to accept his status as tenant and live dependently on his Creator and Lord. But proud man has ambitions beyond his God-given status. He is not satisfied to be a tenant in the Garden of Eden; he wants freehold possession of the Garden of Eden. He is not content with life on God's terms; he believes he can enjoy a better life on his own terms. This false maturity, declares Genesis, this flagrant disobedience of man, is the source of all the chaos, all the confusion, all the misery and all the suffering in which the passing centuries have involved him.

The story of Adam and Eve, which is everlastingly true as the story of man's Fall from God, punctures another of the big illusions of our culture—the illusion of maturity. Specifically the illusion is symbolized by the serpent which the story describes as "more subtle than any beast of the field which the Lord God had made". (Genesis 3:1.) If man thinks he has come of age, it is only because the serpent, which we recognize as a crucial and strikingly modern factor in our culture, encourages him in the illusion. The serpent is that voice in our culture which tempts man, appeals to his pride and incites him to false maturity, the voice which may not express but certainly implies a call to disobedience.[1]

It may be the voice of a psychologist. Consider these observations from a book popular a few years ago, *The Mature Mind*,[2] by Dr Harry Overstreet:

> "Christian religion, as we have known it, took over as its own a premature psychological theory . . . Christianity condemned man to psychological hopelessness . . . It declared him to be basically impotent to work out his psychological salvation. Instead of encouraging him to develop all the characteristically human powers within him and so overcome inner contradictions and outer obstacles, it encouraged him to cast himself on a Power greater than himself . . . and to credit not his own nature, but that mysterious Power, with every virtue that seemed to reside in his own thoughts and behaviours. In short, it encouraged the individual to remain a dependent child. The time is at hand to review the whole situation."

Echoes of a serpent in the Garden of Eden. Not a counsel to disobedience, mind you. The serpent proposed no specific

[1] This is the interpretation of Karl Barth in his *Church Dogmatics*, Vol. 4, *The Doctrine of Reconciliation*, Part I, p. 420ff. T. & T. Clarke, Edinburgh, 1956.

[2] W. W. Newton, New York, 1949.

violation of God's law. It merely insinuated that man might have failed to understand God correctly, or even that God might not understand himself. Can it really be the will of a concerned and intelligent Creator that this magnificent two-legged creature called man, this crown and flower of the evolutionary process, should live for ever in a state of adolescence? More reasonable, surely, that God intends man to come of age, to grow up, to become man in the mature sense of the word, to work out his own salvation and, in a real sense, to be his own god.

Such is the religion of the snake. Call it humanism. But here is a curious thing about humanism: the further a man travels in it, the more inhuman he becomes. Emil Brunner made the novel suggestion that a Doctor of Theology degree be awarded posthumously to Adolph Hitler, because Hitler did more than anybody else to awaken Europe to a consciousness of its Christian heritage by creating a world without Christianity. He showed us with tragic realism that man, when he aspires to be his own god, becomes not only not human but supremely non-human and plunges the world into chaos. Man is a creature, superior to other creatures by virtue of his capacity for friendship with the Creator. Man is made for friendship with God. He can be a man in no other way. If he repudiates this friendship he ceases to be a man and becomes something base and chaotic. Man's maturity is an illusion.

Or it may be the voice of a scientist—not the experimental scientist, humble in his quest for objective truth, but the armchair scientist, one devoted to the methods and procedures of science in a way that rules out other legitimate and necessary devotions such as those implicit in the Christian

Faith. Consider the fantastic claims of Lord Bertrand Russell in his collection of essays published under the provocative title, *Why I am Not a Christian.*[1] Russell can say nothing good about Christianity or about religion at all. He calls religion "a disease born of fear" and tells us that the real antidote to fear is not religion but science. Science, he says, "could teach us no longer to invent allies in the sky, but rather to look on our efforts here below to make this world a fit place to live in, instead of the sort of place the churches in all the centuries have made it." Lord Russell believes that there is "scarcely any limit to what could be done in the way of producing a good world if only men would use science wisely". (He offers no clue as to *how* we shall go about using science wisely.)

"And the serpent was more subtle than any beast of the field which the Lord God had made." So very subtle as he asks what seems like a perfectly straightforward and innocent question: Has God really said that they must not eat the fruit of this particular tree? But this tree bears the most delectable fruit in the garden. Surely there must be some mistake! What kind of God surrounds his creature with all sorts of good things and then denies him the best thing of all? God has made a monkey of man. He has led him by the nose, directed him falsely, pronounced a threat where a supreme promise awaited him. Such a degrading state of affairs cannot continue. Obviously it is time for man to take matters into his own hands, make his own decisions, assume control of his own destiny, be lord of the garden and not a servant.

Such is the religion of the snake, a religion of autonomy and maturity. Proud man listens to it eagerly, not realizing that he is listening to the voice of chaos. What single factor has written sorrier chapters in history than the attempt of

[1] George Allen and Unwin, 1957.

man, who has not the power of lordship over creation, to play the role of lord? True, the prodigious advance in knowledge has invested man with unprecedented power, and we ponder the prediction of an American militarist that whoever puts a human being on the moon will, in fact, control the world. But can we agree with him, agree that knowledge means control when science, our progress in knowledge, has not been accompanied by a corresponding progress in moral forces; when technology, our method of applying knowledge, may be used for destructive as well as constructive purposes; when education, our method of disseminating knowledge, can produce that worst kind of devil, the clever devil; and when politics, the method of organizing knowledge, can be turned to inhuman ends? The message of Eden leaps out at us, the truth that man is essentially and perfectly man only within a relationship of obedience to God. If he revolts against his God-given role and turns it into an undignified farce he becomes not a lord but a slave, the slave of his own destructive passions. Man's maturity is an illusion.

Or it may be the voice of a moralist. In his book, *Existentialism and Humanism*,[1] Jean-Paul Sartre, the French philosopher, simply takes it for granted that thinkers in his school have ceased to believe in the existence of God. For them God is dead. He agrees with Dostoievsky that "if God did not exist, everything would be permitted"; man would be his own judge, the final arbiter of right and wrong. So, indeed, he is, writes Sartre. "Man is nothing else but what he makes of himself", and in this respect each of us contributes to the making of morality and therefore of man. In preferring monogamy to promiscuity, suggests the philosopher, "I am

[1] Methuen and Co., Ltd., London, 1948.

committing not only myself but humanity as a whole to the practice of monogamy. I am thus responsible for myself and for all men, and I am creating a certain image of man as I would have him to be. In fashioning myself, I fashion man."

The serpent in the Garden of Eden was a moral philosopher. "But the serpent said to the woman, 'You will not die. For God knows that when you eat of it your eyes will be opened, and you will be like God, knowing good and evil.'" Does that seem like a fall into immorality? Rather, is it not a rise to genuine morality? That man should know good and evil, that he should take his place at the side of God as arbiter of right and wrong—surely that were a legitimate step forward, man's true development, the evolution of the human race.

Such is the religion of the snake. It seems reasonable and appealing and might be so except that God himself has judged and rejected it. Indeed, think of the chaos, the suffering and the bloodshed which have issued from proud man's self-exaltation to the judgment seat of the universe. Here is another curious thing about man: morally he needs an authority beyond himself. Let him throw his religion away, let him lose the moral reference of Sinai and the Sermon on the Mount, and presently he will find himself doing what once he would have shuddered at. Nazi Germany showed us what a short step it was from the repudiation of God's sovereignty to the extermination of Jews in gas chambers. The truth is that man has not the competence to be his own judge. He can choose between good and evil as God reveals them, but to believe that he himself can make the primary distinction is foolishly to overestimate himself and to let loose in his garden all the forces of hell. Man's maturity is an illusion.

. . .

Or it may be the voice of a dramatist. Samuel Becket's excessively dull play, *Waiting for Godot*, has virtually no plot. Two disgusting, dirty tramps wait under a tree. They wait day after day, year after year, for what? For anything to relieve them of the intolerable burden of existence, the agony of making a decision. Age has withered and habit deadened that divine gift—the human will. They can no longer act, they can only wait, wait for someone else to do the work for them, to take the initiative, wait for a symbolic character who promises but never comes, named Godot. Cynically the playwright has dramatized his philosophy. What a pathetic creature is man—a clown who postures, apes, laughs, cries and crawls, possessed of infinite loneliness! Will man for ever wait supinely for someone to come to his rescue? Will he never learn that God helps only those who help themselves?

Once more an echo of the subtle serpent. Admittedly God has promised to help man in his garden, but is it manly, dignified, mature—this consistent spiritual pauperism, this childish reliance upon grace and mercy from above? Rather, is it not painfully irrational and restrictive? Let man do something. Let him engage in a bold act and eat the forbidden fruit, not as a gesture of defiance but simply to prove that he *is* a man who can stand on his own two feet and who does not have to be thrown back everlastingly upon the help of God.

Such is the religion of the snake, insidiously appealing to proud man in his instinct for independence and his aspiration to maturity: that man should be his own helper. What happened to Adam and Eve, however, is well worth pondering. They did help themselves, they helped themselves to the fruit, and as a result became catastrophically helpless. Adam well typifies world history, for the history of man is indeed the history of his great and fantastic efforts to help himself and, as such, a tragic and chaotic history. Consider again this curious fact about man: while he has made progress he himself is not progressive. Through all the world revolutions wrought by his inventive genius man himself remains basically the same, living in this nuclear age as irrationally as he did in the dark ages, to his own and his neighbour's detriment. In his false maturity it cannot be otherwise, for when man sets out to be his own helper, that is exactly what he has to be. If he will not be helpless before God he can only be helpless abstractly and absolutely, helpless to retrieve his world from chaos. Man's maturity is an illusion.

Here, then, is the timeless truth that leaps out at us from the first book in the Bible. The story of Adam and Eve is no antiquated fable; it is a penetrating, up-to-date diagnosis of our predicament today. Eden represents the world, our world, a God-created garden of peace and plenty which should indeed be a paradise. Adam represents man, modern man, the tenant in the garden who, because he will not obey God and be grateful to him, brings upon himself the inexorable judgment of God that turns his paradise into chaos. The serpent is the beast of chaos, the voice in our culture which tempts man, appeals to his pride and incites him to false maturity, the voice which may not express but certainly implies a call to disobedience.

But we pass from symbol to reality, from poetry to fact when we confront the principal character in the drama, God himself. God has judged proud, sinful man, judged him strangely and marvellously. To the futile attempt of man to become as God, God with infinite condescension has, in fact, become man. To the servant who pretends to be the Lord, God the Lord comes humbly in the form of a servant. In answer to the man who wanted to be his own judge, the Divine Judge offers himself to be judged in our place. To the people who gaily try to help themselves, God appeals from the depths of most utter helplessness, the loneliness and dereliction of a Cross. The gracious God has thrust himself into the midst of our predicament. He has revealed a man's sin in reverse and has shown man's maturity to be an illusion by setting it against the background of real maturity in Jesus Christ of whom the Apostle Paul wrote: "though he was in the form of God, he did not count equality with God a thing to be grasped, but emptied himself, taking the form of a servant, being born in the likeness of men. And being found in human form he humbled himself and became obedient unto death, even death on a cross." (Philippians 2:6–8.) Christ is the New Adam, the Mature Man, God's own answer to the religion of the snake.

Chapter 6

THE ILLUSION OF PROGRESS

"I never expected to live to see what is on the other side of the moon." Those were not the words of a poet but the words of a Canadian astronomer, Dr. Helen Hogg, marvelling at the progress in astronomy made possible by satellites and space travel. There are probably a great many things that she never expected to see within her lifetime—jet aeroplanes, television, penicillin and heart-transplant operations, to mention only a few. We who were born during the past fifty years have been caught up in the most rapid changes in mankind's history. It is true to say that within that comparatively brief period the human race has made more material progress than in all the centuries between the coming of Christ and the middle of the last century. Developments which in the past would have been spread over a thousand years now take place within the lifetime of an individual.

That fact was made visible by the breathtaking exhibits of "Man and His World" at Expo 67 in Montreal. The pavilion "Man the Producer" contained miracles of automation which none of us ever dreamed of seeing in our lifetime. As though television sets and computers were not marvellous enough in themselves, we gaped at a computerized television factory which manufactured sets without evidence of human hands or brain. In the same pavilion there was a chart showing the stages in man's material progress since the dawn of civilization. Centuries, sometimes millenniums separate each distinctive advance, but with the Industrial Revolution the process is accelerated. Then, suddenly, within the period of our lifetime the markings on the chart are squeezed together like an accordion. So it seems almost silly to write about the *illusion* of progress. Anyone with his eyes open to the scientific and technological miracles in the world around him knows that progress is the one thing in modern life that is *not* an illusion.

True enough, but it is also true that progress gives birth to illusions. One of them is *the illusion that progress in the material realm means progress in all realms of life*. That is demonstrably not true, because we know that in some areas man seems to have made no progress at all. Twice in these chapters we have noted as one of man's peculiar features that, though he makes phenomenal progress, he himself is not progressive. Commenting on the failure of man's great and artistic efforts to improve himself as well as his world, Karl Barth compares him to "an unreasoning bullock plodding around in a capstan".

Man's unprogressive nature is one of the recurring themes in the Bible. The Old Testament Book of Judges, presents history as a fascinating drama alive with meaning for the people to whom it was written. To warn them of the consequences of their defection from God the editor puts their history in a nutshell and shows them how each generation passes monotonously through the same five stages: (1) the people worship the Lord and obey him; (2) they forsake the Lord and provoke him to anger; (3) the Lord delivers them into the hands of their enemies; (4) the people are distressed and cry to the Lord for help; (5) the Lord has pity on his people and saves them. Thirteen times the same cycle repeats itself, as though man were indeed an unreasoning bullock plodding around in a capstan, as though history were a trap, a treadmill, a circular grind from which man cannot break loose.

It would seem to confirm the cynicism of the writer of Ecclesiastes who believed quite firmly that there is no progress in the world, no evolution possible, nothing of value transmitted from one person or one generation to another; all things move in a circle accomplishing nothing. "What has been is what will be, and what has been done is what will be done, and there is nothing new under the sun." (Ecclesiastes 1:9.) The Old Testament preacher has plenty of company. Some of the most brilliant scholars, the profoundest philosophers, the greatest historians have subscribed to this cyclical view of history. "Nothing changes!" they tell us. "Everything has happened before. The 'isms' are all 'wasms'. History? It's a drama that repeats itself like one of those old motion pictures that the producers refurbish and throw on a wide screen and try to turn into an epic. The cast is different and the props and the music and the techniques, but the same old plot remains unchanged, and any competent historian can prove it."

Scripture plays a more tragic variation on the theme of man's monotony. In a more sinister sense it shows him to be a creature who is not progressive. The New Testament Book of Revelation communicates Divine truth through the medium of visions which, when we probe the reality behind them, speak an awesome Word of God to our day. At one point in the drama seven successive angels blow their trumpets to herald God's judgment on the evil of the world, and seven successive catastrophes of gathering intensity befall the human race. A third of the earth is scorched by fire, a third of the sea turned to blood, a third of the world plunged into darkness; then comes a plague of scorpions followed by an invasion of 200 million cavalry, their horses breathing fire, smoke and sulphur, snuffing out a third of mankind. Only a remnant of the earth's population remains, yet even of this remnant we read these sombre words: "The rest of mankind who survived these plagues still did not abjure the gods their hands had fashioned, nor cease their worship of devils and of idols made from gold, silver, bronze, stone, and wood, which cannot see or hear or walk. Nor did they repent of their murders, their sorcery, their fornication, or their robberies." (Revelation 9:20–21.)

We never learn, do we? That is the grim truth which the author of Revelation communicates through his series of bizarre visions. He is telling us that the catastrophes of history teach us nothing, and history itself seems to validate that truth. As for material progress, it only exaggerates our stupidities and complicates our problems. If progress in the material realm did mean progress in all realms of life, we should be the most enlightened, most humane, most peaceful generation in the world's history and we should compare with the ancients as a prayer meeting compares with a pack of fighting dogs. Yet it was not ancient Rome but one of the most civilized countries in modern times that slaughtered six million Jews in concentration camps; not only ancient Greece but a twentieth-century power that taxes its people to prosecute an unpopular foreign war; not in the Dark Ages but in this modern age that men defeat their enemies by starving them to death. At the very dawn of history a man murdered his brother and, when God held him accountable, he retorted,

"Am I my brother's keeper?" (Genesis 4:9.) Apparently we have not progressed beyond *that*!

Another illusion to which progress gives birth is *the illusion that we have nothing to learn from the past*. There was a tense and dramatic moment at the 1968 Convocation of the University of Toronto. When one of the graduates appeared on the platform to receive his diploma he asked the Chancellor if he could say a few words. The ushers immediately tried to remove him, but the Acting President said that he could have the microphone for two minutes. Before that dignified assembly the student stood on the stage of Convocation Hall and shouted at his fellow-graduates, "Fellow niggers, look what Mr. Charlie's done to your minds." Then to the accompaniment of loud boos and hisses, with only a scattering of applause, he tore up his Bachelor of Arts diploma and marched out of the building. In that one juvenile gesture this young man, who was vice-president of the Ontario Union of Students, consigned to the scrap-heap all that the university had given him.

He was not altogether untypical. In fact, he represents a generation of young people so conditioned by sports cars and space travel that they look down their noses not only on the horse-and-coach days but on many of the values and traditions of the horse-and-coach days. They are religious in their own way; they worship at the cult of the contemporary. They re-date history not with the coming of Christ but the coming of themselves. They take the attitude that history began yesterday and that all that went before belongs to primeval times. "We are the people," they say confidently, "the generation of the first enlightened age. All who went before us, all who have been in the world for more than thirty years are dead. The past? Forget about it! The past has nothing to teach us!" Such is another of the illusions of progress.

But it *is* an illusion. Any fool ought to know, and certainly any young man with a higher education ought to know that life does not begin all over again with any one generation. Life is more like a relay race where you take what's handed to you, run as fast as you can and hand it on to your children. Even the rebellious graduate would surely concede that not all the books in the university library were written last week. Some were written last year, and some the year before that; there may be some that were written a few centuries ago. Even he would admit that experiments in the science laboratories do not start from scratch but take as their starting-point the results of experiments made in the past. Even he would surely admit that people over thirty must know a few things, else we should not have built the university and we should not have the enlightened social conscience to pay the taxes which keep him in university. G. K. Chesterton defined tradition as "giving the vote to that most obscure of all classes, our ancestors", as "refusing to submit to the small and arrogant oligarchy of those who are walking about".The wise man is the man who acknowledges gratefully that in all areas of life—in science, literature, morality, religion—we do have ancestors who bequeathed to us a thing or two of enduring value.

Some proponents of the "new morality" seem to labour under the illusion that we have nothing to learn from the past. Their whole point of view is identical with that of the university graduate who tore up his diploma. "New times demand new morality," they say, and promptly toss on the scrap-heap the accumulated wisdom of the ages. They seem curiously unaware of the fact that what they offer as a "new morality" is not moral and certainly not new; it has been tried many times before and rejected because it simply won't work. In the United States there is a loose organization known as the National Organization of Women (N.O.W.) that proposes to abolish marriage, thus giving a man and woman the right to conjugal love and the procreation of children without having to live together and establish a home. Don't they know that it has been tried before? Don't they know that in its long history mankind has tried every conceivable experiment with the sex relationship—polyandry, polygamy, monogamy, promiscuity, wives, concubines, mistresses and prostitutes—and that there is, in fact, no basically new arrangement which has not been tried? Don't they know that through all this long experimenting of the race a single behaviour pattern continually rises to the top as the requisite of human well-being and happiness—the pattern of a man and a woman loving each other so much that they do not care to love anybody else in the same way, a man and a woman building a permanent home that puts around the children the strong security of an unbroken affection? That is what the past has to teach us, and we are stupid not to learn from it.

There was a preacher who announced as his Sunday sermon subject, "Which Way Is Progress?" Later in the week a friend asked him, "What did you say from the pulpit? Which way *is* progress?" The preacher replied, "Sometimes it is backwards." The friend persisted, "When is progress backwards?" He received the answer, "Progress is backwards when you have wandered away from home."

That is one of the great lessons of the Bible and especially of the Hebrew prophets who, though they were liberals in the best sense of the word, were also conservatives in the best sense of the word. With daring they pointed men to the future but with wisdom they also pointed them to the past. Fearlessly they broke with outworn traditions but with equal courage they tried to preserve traditions which ought to be preserved. They blazed new trails and at the same time counselled men to follow the ancient paths. So Jeremiah: "Thus says the Lord: Stand by the roads, and look, and ask for the ancient paths, where the good way is; and walk in it and find rest for your souls." (Jeremiah 6:16.) The prophet was telling his own people, as he now tells us, that even through a new country in time there are some ancient paths, familiar trails beaten down by the footprints of men who learned from experience and taught us the secret of successful living, and that it is an illusion to suppose that with all our material progress we can find easier and safer ways. "Thou shalt not kill . . . Thou shall not steal . . . Honour thy father and thy mother . . . Blessed are the meek . . . the merciful . . . the peacemakers . . . the pure in heart . . ." We have not progressed beyond *that*!

A third illusion to which progress gives birth is *the illusion that nothing is permanent, nothing survives all change.* That is demonstrably an illusion for the very reason that some things have survived the changes of the centuries. One has only to read history and biography to see that certain values are essentially as important today as they were in ancient times. Suppose we take the Old Testament as our reference. Nearly 4,000 years ago a pioneer named Abraham emigrated to an unknown destination, propelled by the faith that he would eventually reach his destination. Is that so very different from the faith which propels cosmonauts into outer space? Five centuries before the Christian era the exiled Jews in Babylon expressed their hope of return by singing, "When the Lord turned again the captivity of Zion ..." (Psalm 126:1.) Is that so very different from the hope of American Negroes who sing, "We shall overcome"? In an earlier period a Hebrew mother saved her beloved baby from the fury of Pharaoh by hiding him in the bulrushes. Is that so very different from Hebrew mothers who saved their beloved babies from the fury of Hitler by hiding them in cellars? Faith, hope, love—the Apostle Paul said that these are values which last for ever.

Shortly after World War Two an American newspaper man interviewed the Mayor of Canterbury. Living there, amidst those historic surroundings which were still scarred by fire that fell from the skies, the Mayor had developed a strangely serene outlook toward the terrifying trend of world events. "Communism! Russia!" he said. "They will be topics of medieval history which students will be flunking 800 years from now." Beginning with the campaigns of Caesar, he catalogued the almost countless occasions in history when old Canterbury has been the scene of invasion and warfare. Then, pointing to the world-famous Cathedral, he said, "Still it stands. Still men worship within its walls. Still they work and love and play. They will love and play and work and worship centuries from now."

There is a world of computers, and there is a world of cathedrals. God's Word punctures the illusion of progress by telling us that we are citizens of both these worlds: the one a visible, fluctuating, transient world; the other an invisible, constant, imperishable world; the one a world of revolution, the other a world of revelation; the one a source of unrest and anxiety, the other a source of quietness and stability; the one a world of the body, the other a world of the spirit. These two worlds, both real, both under God's sovereignty, come together in Jesus Christ, God's incarnate Word; and to live in Christ is to live in both worlds, facing up to the challenge of one, yet finding in the other our source of sanity and peace.

It is possible that a time of rapid material progress brings more sharply into focus the Divine values which were incarnate in Christ. That was the conviction of the New Testament writer of the Epistle to the Hebrews who lived in a day not unlike our own when the world about him was changing like a kaleidoscope. A level-headed man, he told his readers not to panic but to keep calm and realize that the storms which shake our lives to the very foundations are often intended to release us from our reliance on the superficial, conventional values in order that we may see clearly and pin our faith on those eternal, abiding values that no wind of change can ever shake. He went further and pleaded with his readers to believe that the upheaval and confusion of life was no accident but the purposeful activity of God. Speaking for God, he said, "Yet once more I shake not the earth only but also heaven . . . signifying the removing of those things that are shaken . . . that those things which cannot be shaken may remain." (Hebrews 12:26, 27.)

Of course, these are truths which cannot be argued; they can only be enforced and illustrated. We saw an illustration at the New York World's Fair where a torpedo-shaped capsule was sunk three hundred feet in the ground presumably to be discovered five thousand years from now. It contained a variety of objects which will enable men in the year 6965 to document our civilization as it was in the year 1965. One tries to imagine their reaction. They may wonder, for example, what we did with a tiny scrap of cloth known as a bikini and how our eardrums stood the raucous noice of a gramophone record made by some insects known as the Beatles. A transistor radio, a plastic heart valve and a computer memory unit will tell them that we made marvellous material progress, but tranquillizer pills and filter cigarettes may indicate that we were not too progressive. Most of the objects in the capsule will seem dated and totally strange to them, and they may wonder if we valued anything from the past. Then they will find a book which, we dare to believe, will be as familiar to our descendants as it is to us and as it was to our ancestors. In that book they will read a prayer: "Lord, thou hast been our dwelling place in all generations. Before the mountains were brought forth, or ever thou hadst formed the earth and the world, even from everlasting to everlasting thou art God." (Psalm 90:1–2.) We have not progressed beyond *that*!

CHAPTER 7

THE ILLUSION OF INSIGNIFICANCE

A novel which was published a few years ago bears as its title the single, significant and suggestive word, *One*.[1] It is a chilling story that projects us into a future totalitarian State where all men spy upon one another and where no one is secure. A university professor named Burden is arrested, not for breaking the law but because a routine investigation shows that he has a sense of his own personal worth. He thinks of himself as an individual, and *that* is heresy in a totalitarian State. Instead of ordering Burden to be liquidated, the prosecutor decides to make him a guinea-pig. He will pulverize this man's soul, destroy his sense of identity and prove that the human personality can be scientifically reduced from one to zero.

So Burden is imprisoned and subjected to a succession of horrible physical and psychological tortures from which he emerges a shadow of his former self, having no memories of his past, his name, his family or his profession. He goes back into the world a beaten, timid little man with the new name of Hughes, ready to take a minor post in the civil service and lose his identity in that of the State. The satanic plot has

[1] David Karp, *One*, Grosset & Dunlap, 1962, New York.

succeeded. Or has it? One day the genial gentleman who keeps an eye on the experiment comes to the prosecutor with the disturbing report that Hughes, while he conforms to collectivism, still thinks of himself as an individual, as *the* Hughes, the only Hughes. The prosecutor, beside himself with rage, orders the execution of his guinea-pig, grudgingly admitting that in this world nothing short of death can reduce the human personality from one to zero.

David Karp, the author of *One*, has not written for our entertainment. He is one of the secular preachers of our time, speaking to us through the medium of fiction; and we can thank God that the world still listens to preachers, if not inside the Church, then outside of it. Karp is one of several modern novelists crusading for the rights of the individual in a day when creeping collectivism jeopardizes those rights and threatens to reduce the human personality from one to zero. These novelists are protesting against a dangerous trend in all parts of the world, even in countries that boast of their democratic way of life. The inherent danger of that trend is expressed by a Latin phrase, *corruptio optimi pessima*—"the worst is but the corruption of the best". When any human good is clutched and cherished and made the sovereign good it may turn to evil and produce its opposite. The great good that we are being told to work and sacrifice for these days is the common good, the good of society—and no Christian will deny that it is a worthy goal consistent with the highest Christian ideals—but society, if we treat it as the ultimate good, can become the enemy of man instead of his friend; it can depersonalize man, dehumanize him and make him a slave of the state.

David Karp, Ayn Rand and other novelists have set themselves to puncture another of the great illusions of our culture.

It is the illusion that society is everything and the individual is nothing. It is the illusion that the individual no longer counts in the scheme of things, an illusion promoted by the collectivists, encouraged by science and technology, and believed by multitudes of ordinary people who feel their personalities pulverized into insignificance by the organized, mechanized, computerized, standardized character of modern life. It is the illusion of insignificance—the mistaken idea that in the perspective of eternity a man does not matter; he is an insect, indistinguishable from the mass of insects, and therefore of lesser importance than the society to which he belongs, the earth on which he lives and the very machines which he has helped to create.

It is surely strange that secular writers, some of whom are professed agnostics and even atheists, sometimes speak more prophetically to the depersonalizing elements in our culture than do the spokesmen of organized religion. The Church ought to be saying what David Karp and his fellow-novelists are saying because the Church, if it preserves the integrity of the Gospel, knows full well the infinite value and sacredness of human personality in the sight of God. The Church, if its mind were instructed less by the pronouncements of social action committees and more by the Word of God, could speak to "organization man" a word that would puncture his illusion of insignificance and restore his sense of dignity and worth as an individual. But the Church must speak with conviction and authority. It must speak not from books but from *The Book*. The Bible exalts human personality as earth's greatest treasure. In the Bible no man is ever merged in the mass of men. In the sight of God each man is always the only man.

. . .

When you open the Bible at its very first chapter you read these words, "God created man in his own image." (Genesis 1:27.) All else had been completed—day and night, earth and sky, beast and fowl, tree and flower. And God surveyed his creation experiment and saw that it was good. Only the climax remained. Somewhere back in the millennia God said, "Now I will fashion a new order of being. I shall call him MAN. He will differ from all my other creatures not only in degree but in kind. To him I will give reason, intelligence, the faculty of creating and appreciating beauty, a moral sense, the ability to distinguish between right and wrong and the freedom to choose right or wrong. He shall be the lord of my creation, my agent upon earth. He shall work with me and enjoy friendship with me. He shall be to me as a son to a father; and, to make that relationship possible, I shall make him like myself and give him what I alone possess—eternal personality."

"God created man *in his own image*". Ponder that last phrase. It means that man, every man, is a child of God. He is not a thing, though his body obeys the laws of physics; not an animal, though his organism responds to biological impulses. Within the blood and brains and sinew of each human being God has ignited an original spark of Divinity that no one, not even a state prosecutor, can snuff out save by extinguishing the everlasting fire of God himself.

"God created man in his own image"—not *men* but *man*. As André Gide wrote in his *Journal*, "Man is more interesting than men. God made *him* and not them in his image. Each one is more precious than all." From the treasure-house of the Jewish Talmud comes this wise commentary:

"Why did God create only one Adam and not many at a

time? He did this to demonstrate that one man in himself is an entire universe. Also he wished to teach mankind that he who kills one human being is as guilty as if he had destroyed the entire world. Similarly, he who saves the life of one single human being is as worthy as if he had saved all humanity . . . When a maker of coins does his work he uses only one mould and all the coins emerge alike. But the King of kings, blessed be His name, has created all mankind in the mould of Adam, and even so no man is identical to another. For this reason each person must respect himself and say with dignity: 'God created the world on my account. Therefore let me not lose eternal life because of some vain passion!"

Open the Bible at some of the Old Testament Psalms. One of them is suggested by Henry Sloane Coffin when he writes of a little ritual through which William Beebe, the naturalist, and President Theodore Roosevelt used to go. After an evening's chat they would step outside and look up at the heavens. Searching, with or without the aid of a telescope, until they found the faint spot of light-mist at the lower left-hand corner of the great square of Pegasus, one of them would recite: "That is the Spiral Galaxy of Andromeda. It is as large as our Milky Way. It is one of a hundred million galaxies. It is seven hundred and fifty thousand light years away. It consists of one hundred billion suns, each larger than our sun." After an interval Roosevelt would grin and say, "Now I think we feel small enough! Let's go to bed."[1]

But see another man's reaction to the same celestial immensity. Five centuries before Christ, a Hebrew poet stood on the Judean hills and stared up at the night sky, the moon and

[1] Henry Sloane Coffin, *Communion Through Preaching*, Charles Scribner's Sons, Ltd., New York and London, 1952, pp. 16–17

stars and the glittering galaxies in heaven above. The vastness and variety of the stellar universe staggers him, but what staggers him even more is the thought that God, who brought the worlds into being, does for him what he does not do for all the planets and solar systems. He is mindful of him and visits him. He loves him with an everlasting love.

> "When I consider thy heavens, the work of thy fingers, the moon and stars which thou hast ordained; What is man that thou art mindful of him . . . ?" (Psalm 8:3, 4.)

The psalmist cannot resist the belief that there must be something behind this Divine visitation, something which lifts him above nature, above heredity and environment, even above the history which has helped to make him. However wonderful the stars, they can never be so wonderful, never so precious in the sight of God as one human eye that beholds the stars, one human brain that measures them. Astronomically-speaking, man is not a speck of dust; he is the astronomer. Dwarfed by the cosmic universe, a single man is still in a spiritual sense the centre of the cosmic universe, the crown of God's creation, lower only than God himself.

Or turn to the 139th Psalm. It is the soliloquy of a man who has made an astonishing discovery—the discovery that, however insignificant a person may be in his own eyes or in the eyes of society, he is not insignificant to God. The Hebrew poet is so completely overcome with a sense of God's personal concern for him that there seem to be only two people in the universe—himself and God. Out of a full heart he cries: "God knows all about me, my past, present and future. He knows me by name. He considers the smallest detail of my life. He knows the purposes of my mind even before they take thought-form. God not only knows; he cares. He made his plans for me when I was in my mother's womb." The psalmist does not understand how God, with a whole universe to care for, can be interested in one human being, nor does he try to understand. He admits that such infinite knowledge is too wonderful for his finite mind to grasp. He is very certain, however, that God does care for him and that nowhere in time, space or eternity can a single child of God escape from the Father's pursuing love.

It is when we come to the New Testament and the teachings of Jesus that we really begin to understand how precious is the individual in the sight of God. Jesus believed, as no one before him had ever believed, in the all-surpassing worth of personality. He believed that the whole world cannot be set in the balance over against one human soul. That belief shines in everything he says and does. It looks out from his eyes when they are happiest and when they are saddest. It trembles in the most loving consolations and thunders in the most passionate rebukes that leave his lips. It is the inspiration at once of his pity and his indignation. "The sabbath was made for man, not man for the sabbath" (Mark 2:27), he admonished the watch-dogs of religious orthodoxy. Daringly Jesus taught that even the loftiest institutions and regulations of religion must always take second place to the interests of people. So must the State and democracy and law and labour and culture and education and science and industry and all other systems and organizations of men which gobble up the individual and threaten to destroy his identity. In God's value scale these are the servants not the masters of the human soul and they should be modified, waived or ignored when they conflict with the soul's welfare.

The ministry of Jesus in the New Testament was supremely a ministry not to social structures but to individuals. He was always stopping to help them, always turning his attention from the many to the one. In Capernaum one day he and the disciples pushed their way through a great crowd of people on a life-or-death errand. Suddenly the Master felt a hand on his garment. "Who was it that touched me?" he asked, turning around. Impatiently the disciples retorted, "Master, the multitudes surround you and press upon you." (Luke 8:45.) But Jesus didn't see the multitudes. He saw one person, a woman, one needy, suffering soul in that vast throng. In that moment not another person in the world mattered to him. There was a day in Jericho when he heard the cry of a blind beggar above the shouts of the crowd; and for the sake of that one lowly individual, that cipher in the social scale, Jesus stopped. (Luke 18:40.) He stopped. It was God's way of saying to the humblest person, lost in the crowd and swallowed by society, "You count! I am concerned about you."

Jesus did not claim to be God in human form, but he did say to his disciples, "He who has seen me has seen the Father." He also said, "I am the good shepherd" and he gave this picture of a good shepherd: "What man of you, having a hundred sheep . . . does not leave the ninety-nine in the wilderness, and go after the one which is lost, until he finds it?" (Luke 15:4.) That picture, familiar in first century Palestine, came alive for me on a day when my family and I climbed Mount Snowdon in North Wales. It was springtime, and the streams were swollen. On the far bank of one of them we suddenly saw a new-born lamb huddled helplessly in a hollow of ground. The girls and I remained there while my wife walked farther up the mountain to a farmhouse. After a while she returned with the farmer who tenderly and joyously picked up the animal and cradled it in his arm as if it were a human baby. In his lilting Welsh voice he thanked us and said, "I have been looking for this lamb for two days." That is a picture of what God thinks of the individual. So high does personality rate in God's value scale that, like a shepherd leaving the rest of his flock while he searches for a single stray, God is prepared to let the whole universe run itself while he seeks the salvation of one human soul. All Heaven's energies sometimes focus on one lost individual, and the angels sing when God in Christ finds and brings him safely home.

Jesus himself—not only his teachings, his miracles and his ministry, but Jesus himself—is the Word of God that punctures the illusion of insignificance. No man can look at Jesus and say that the individual does not matter to God. Jesus is the supreme proof of the place of a person in God's scale of values and in God's scheme for the whole creation. When God, whom man had never seen, wanted to reveal himself fully and completely to men, he chose as his revelation not a cataclysm of nature but a man who was bone of our bone and flesh of our flesh. When God, who presides over history, wanted his grace and truth to break into history with undying radiance and power, he chose as his interpreter not a line of kings or a school of philosophers but the son of a peasant maiden and a village carpenter. When God, whom the world had defied, wanted to save the world from destroying itself, he chose as the world's Saviour not a system, an organization, an ideology, but that which in all the universe he rates most infinitely precious—a single human personality.

One! We can take that terse title from David Karp's book and apply it to every book in the Bible. Against the dangerous trend of modern life to pulverize personality the Bible thunders its eternal protest. It warns our civilization that to underrate the value of one human being is to call God a fool for having created man in his own image, for being mindful of him beyond all the rest of creation, for making him an object of infinite concern, and for redeeming him through the teaching, ministry and person of the man, Jesus. But God is no fool, and the civilization that treats him as such has written its own obituary.

The Bible warns us that whoever thinks of another person as less than one not only insults that person but blasphemes the Holy Name of God. It warns us that whoever thinks of himself as less than one not only depreciates himself but blasphemes the Holy Name of God. To each one of us the Bible comes up and says, "Don't sell yourself short. You're not a nobody. You are somebody. If you were the only living creature in this universe you would still be more important than the universe itself. No constellation, no computer, no government, no political or economic theory can compare with you. You are unique, distinctive. God never created anyone like you before and he never will again. Whatever you may think of yourself, whatever society may think of you, you are infinitely precious to God."

On a cold January morning in 1965 the dignitaries of the earth assembled in one place. Monarchs, princes, presidents and prime ministers from all countries gathered under the roof of a Christian church; and while they bowed their heads, the whole world kept silence. It was as though time stood still for the space of half-an-hour. What brought the great and mighty together? They did not come to gaze at the heavens through a telescope, or to marvel at some miracle of modern science, or to witness a coronation, or to celebrate a military victory, or to inaugurate a movement for world peace. They came to thank God for a man, one man whose unique life has been synonymous with the history of the twentieth century in all its glory and catastrophe. His intellectual and artistic genius, his great gifts of mind and heart, his power to lead and inspire were more phenomenal than any constellation, any computer, any government, any political or economic theory. No superlatives can express what the human race owes to that one man—Sir Winston Churchill. Beyond all the tributes that were paid to him it can be said that he showed the whole world the greatness, the grandeur, the eternal significance of one human personality created in the image of God.

CHAPTER 8

THE ILLUSION OF FUTILITY

"Barbed-wire sickness" was a name coined by French doctors for a disease which appeared in prison camps during World War One. Herbert Farmer writes about it in one of his books.[1] Its chief symptom was a depressed and hollow feeling of the futility of human existence. Whatever he picked up—books tools, musical instruments—the prisoner of war soon threw them down and exclaimed hopelessly, "What's the use anyway?" "So it is with the human spirit today," writes Dr. Farmer. "It has barbed-wire sickness."

As a sickness the feeling of futility usually sets in somewhere during middle-age. In youth a man blazes with idealism. He approaches life with the confidence of a crusader. He believes that the world can be improved and that he can do something to improve it. With advancing years, however, he realizes that, though he has done his best, the world remains pretty much the same, and he begins to suspect that his youthful ideals were a childish illusion. If the structure of civilization is on fire, his small bucket of water won't extinguish it, so he throws down the bucket and retreats into the shell of his creature comforts, leaving the salvation of the world to the younger generation.

[1] H. H. Farmer, *The Servant of the Word,* Nisbet and Co. Ltd., London, 1941. p. 133.

There is much in our modern world to encourage the feeling of futility. In the summer of 1968, when the Russians invaded Czechoslovakia, we saw television pictures made in the streets of Prague. People were hurrying past a huge Russian tank standing near Wenceslas Square. One of them, who appeared to be wearing running-shoes, suddenly paused and kicked one of the massive tracks of the military monster. It illustrated, as well as anything could, the futility of one person struggling against cold steel, the futility of the individual pitting his frail strength against the massive machines of militarism and power politics that ride roughshod over the human spirit.

Many voices in our culture encourage the feeling of futility. A few years ago the British Broadcasting Corporation presented a frightening television drama, entitled "A Fable", which showed the problem of racism in reverse. We saw a Black Power society where white people suffered the discriminations, the indignities, the privations and the persecutions that they now visit on people with coloured skins. The most pathetic figure in this upside-down drama was a Negro intellectual who wrote pamphlets and newspaper articles from the comfort of his home protesting against the prejudice of his people and demanding justice for all men whom God had created equal. What he didn't know (or perhaps he did know) was that his writings were never published, not even delivered, because the messenger took them directly to the basement and burned them in the furnace. So much for the idealists, the crusaders and the do-gooders in our world!

But suppose we turn a deaf ear to the voices in our culture and listen instead to a few of the voices speaking from the Bible, what do *they* tell us? They tell us that futility is at best an illusion and at worst an excuse for cowardly inaction. They tell us that improving the world is not as simple as improving a piece of property. You can't bulldoze away the rubbish and tear up the weeds and turn a wilderness into a lovely garden in a single summer. You can labour for a life-time and never see the results of your labours. But there will be results. No good thing is ever lost, and the efforts of one decent man, dedicated to the common good, will make a difference.

Listen, first, to *the voice of an Old Testament prophet*. His name was Isaiah, and he prophesied at a critical juncture in his people's history when the fire of God's righteousness had miraculously consumed their enemies. That same fire would consume them, if they did not begin building a fireproof society, a society that would be morally immune to the spirit of burning. Isaiah describes that society. He holds it as a vision before his people. It will be a world of righteousness; a world where governments exist not to be served but to serve; a world where people are morally mature, discerning the difference between right and wrong, choosing the right instead of the wrong; a world of human equality where artificial class distinctions disappear and where the ruling aristocracy is the aristocracy of character.

Isaiah goes further. He tells his people what the shelter and fountain-force of an ideal society must be—not knowledge, not material wealth, not political power, not military might, not crowns and thrones—but men. The secret of a strong society always has been and always will be the strength and freshness of individual human personality. So declares the prophet in words which are indelibly inscribed in the human conscience: "And a man shall be as a hiding place from the wind and covert from the tempest; as rivers of water in a dry place, as the shadow of a great rock in a weary land." (Isaiah 32:2.)

Isaiah's great interpreter, Sir George Adam Smith, reminds us that the prophet drew his imagery from the desert which he knew so well. He had seen the desert wind pile up the dunes like the waves of the sea, engulfing and blotting out all plant life. The only thing that could arrest the drift was a great rock. Behind its bulwark life was safe from the smothering sand. Smith reminds us that it is in this sense that men can serve the common good. Deadly forces, as blind and fatal as the desert sand, sweep down history, but one man serves his nation and the human race by acting as a rock and arresting the drift, and a whole generation finds shelter under his shadow.

Someone has said that "the history of what man has accomplished in the world is at bottom the history of the great men who have worked there". That is certainly true of Bible history. Through the pages of Scripture sweep the deadly drifts of paganism, superstition and barbarism, but at intervals the drift stops suddenly, arrested by one man, an Abraham, a Moses, an Isaiah, a rock-like character whom God raised up to be a shelter for all his people. It is true of the Church's history. Every great reformation, every new awakening of faith, every significant Christian advance can trace its origins to one individual, an Augustine, a Francis, a Luther, a Wesley, a single rock-like character who set his will, strong through faith, against prevailing tendencies and became a shelter for all his people. It is true of modern political history which, though swept by the drifts of corruption, injustice, prejudice, poisonous custom and dust-laden controversy, has again and again been saved by the emergence of a Lincoln, a

Gandhi, a Churchill, a Kennedy, a rock-like leader to arrest those drifts and to be a shelter for all his people.

The longest, heaviest drift in history, which smothers every effort of man to improve his world, is man's inborn cussedness to which the Bible gives the old-fashioned name of "sin". Men have tried to stop it with government, education, science, philosophy and religion, but sin, like a driving sand storm, has smothered them all. Only Christ resisted sin, and only those who cling to him can be safe from its deadly drift. That is the good news of the Gospel. That is why the word of God's prophet contains more than a philosophy of history; it contains a promise that God fulfilled when he raised up a man to arrest radically the drift of evil and to be as a Rock under whose shadow succeeding generations have found shelter and life. Christ is history's supreme example of the power of one person to change and shape history. He is God's own answer to the illusion of futility.

Listen, then, to *the voice of Jesus*. He talked not only of improving this world. He gave us a grander and more magnificent view of world society than the most daring social idealist would ever dare to dream, a society so in harmony with the will of God and so obedient to the laws of God that it can be described only as the Kingdom of God. He said that he himself represented that Kingdom, that he was the embodiment of the perfect relationship between God as King and man as subject which is God's plan for society. Jesus taught that the Kingdom as a social reality will come completely at the end of history as a gift from God. Yet he also taught that the Kingdom comes gradually within history as men work for it here and now. And he taught *how* it comes. He gave us two unforgettable figures of speech which if we take them seriously, save us from the illusion of futility.

Jesus said, "The Kingdom of God is like a grain of mustard seed . . . it is the smallest of the seeds, but when it has grown it . . . becomes a tree . . ." (Matthew 13:31–32.) It is a way of saying that the Kingdom of God has small beginnings, and who has a greater right to proclaim that truth than Jesus himself? The secular historian, Hendrik van Loon, writes in his *Story of Mankind*:[1] "It was the 753rd year since the founding of Rome. Gaius Julius Caesar Octavinius Augustus was living in the palace on the Palatine Hill busily engaged upon the task of ruling his Empire . . . In a little village of distant Syria, Mary, the wife of Joseph the Carpenter, was tending her little boy born in a stable of Bethlehem . . . This is a strange world . . . Before long, the palace and the stable were to meet in open combat . . . And the stable was to emerge victorious." Yes, a strange world, because the God who created and governs it is a God of small beginnings. He begins to change history and turn the world upside-down in the smallest, quietest, most unobtrusive way—with the birth of a baby in a barn.

We can thank God that not all the voices in our secular culture encourage the illusion of futility. In one of his books[2] Dr John Robinson quotes from the novel, *Incognito*, written by the Rumanian ex-Communist, Petru Dumitriu. The hero of the novel is imprisoned and subjected to utter dehumanizing degradation and torture. He is made to suffer unbearable pain. Yet, even while "the screams issued mechanically from his ill-used body", even while his captors

[1] Harrap and Co., Ltd., 1961.
[2] John A. T. Robinson, *Exploration into God,* Stanford University Press, Stanford, California, 1967, pp. 91–96

crushed him like an insect under their feet, he refused to hate them, refused to lose faith in God and man. Indeed, he saw their faces, however terrifying and sad, as the face of God. He saw all faces, all persons, all things, all events as the 'incognitos' of God and he knew that he had to love them even as they were. He said, "If I love the world as it is, I am already changing it: a first fragment of the world has been changed, and that is my own heart." When you believe that the smallest fragment of the world can be changed, even though that fragment is only your own heart, you will not throw up your hands in despair and give way to the illusion of futility.

Jesus gave another figure of speech: "The Kingdom of God is like leaven which a woman took and hid in three measures of meal, till it was all leavened." (Matthew 13:33.) This yeasty figure conveys the truth that vitality is mightier than size and as such it offers a valuable corrective to our thinking in these days when life has become so victimized by bigness, so mechanized, organized, standardized and computerized that man himself seems to be no more than a meaningless cipher. It is true that one decent person can do precious little to influence the vast systems of business, politics, industry and culture that make for prosperity or poverty, freedom or tyranny, righteousness or corruption, peace or war. It is also true, however, and a fact of history, that in every age the determinative factors are not the vociferous affairs that split the eardrums of contemporaries but human forces, embryonic, secretive, often imperceptible to the majority. Vital persons, vital groups, vital ideas—these are the forces that influence civilization.

Albert Schweitzer once said, "However much concerned I am with the problem of evil in the world, I never let myself get lost in broodings on it. I always hold firmly to the thought that each one of us can do a little to bring some portion of it to an end." Schweitzer himself was a living example of the truth that vitality is mightier than size. His jungle hospital at Lambaréné seemed small and insignificant compared with the wars and revolutions and power politics that sway the trend of events in modern Africa, but men did not go to see his hospital, they went to see Schweitzer himself. This human genius, philosopher, theologian, musician and doctor, dedicating his life to the healing of Africans in primitive surroundings, exercised as mighty an influence on the human conscience as any man of this century. Journalists and adventurers did not always understand the motives behind Schweitzer's astounding career of self-renunciation and service, yet they knew and admitted that in a remote corner of Africa was force stronger and more lasting than all the tyrannies and machines and missiles and nuclear weapons of our modern age. Dictators and revolutionaries may change the political pattern overnight, but in the long run it will be the Schweitzers who change the hearts of men and, therefore, the course of history.

The Quakers have a motto: "It is better to light one candle than to curse the darkness." It is a good motto because it sums up the truth of what Jesus said about the mustard seed and the leaven; and there is always the possibility that other people will light candles, and the world's darkness give way to a mighty flame brighter than the noon-day sun. At least, when you light a candle you can see where you are going and you can keep going. You don't have to wring your hands and stand still, and that alone saves you from the illusion of futility.

. . . . .

Next, we listen to *the voice of the Apostle Paul* in the fifteenth chapter of his First Letter to the Corinthians. It is a remarkable chapter when we recall the character of Corinth, that tough sea-port town in southern Greece which in Paul's day was a cesspool of lust and corruption. Living the Christian life and trying to promote the Kingdom of God in Corinth must have seemed as futile as trying to kill a sabre-toothed tiger with a fly-swatter, and there must have been times when the Corinthian Christians felt tempted to quit in despair. Yet to those Christians Paul wrote: "Therefore, my beloved brethren, be steadfast, unmovable, always abounding in the work of the Lord, knowing that in the Lord your labour is not in vain." (I Corinthians 15:58.)

The key-word is "therefore", a bridge-word in Paul's letters, indicating that what he is about to say is predicated on what he has just been saying. So we have to listen to the whole of this chapter which is constructed like a symphony. It begins with a mighty affirmation of Christ's resurrection from the dead—a fact of history supported by many reliable witnesses, including Paul himself. Then it moves to the quieter tones of philosophical argument, leading us to see that resurrection is not just a possibility but the only reasonable hope both for Christ and for ourselves. After that, the statement of fact again from which Paul draws out the moral implications of immortality for the individual and for human history. Then, back to reasoned argument about the nature of the resurrection body, this time mounting to a crescendo until it reaches a climax in Paul's daring defiance of Death, "O death, where is thy sting? O grave, where is thy victory?", and the shout of triumph, "Thanks be to God who gives us the victory through our Lord Jesus Christ!" Then and only then, in the flush of victory and with the strains of the resurrection symphony ringing in his ears, can Paul say stoutly, "Therefore, my beloved brethren, be steadfast, unmovable, always abounding in the work of the Lord, knowing that in the Lord your labour is not in vain."

No Christian who believes that God raised Jesus Christ from the dead can succumb to the illusion of futility. No Christian who hopes that he will share Christ's resurrection can throw up his hands in the face of the world's evil and cry out, "What's the use of trying to change it?" To be sure, he feels a sense of futility at times, just as Paul may have felt it as he pursued his perilous missionary journeys through the ancient world. What impact could he, one dedicated man, possibly have on the unyielding power structure of the Roman Empire with its entrenched evils and pagan practices? Yet Paul never asked that irrelevant question. He simply offered his service to God. He knew that improving the world is God's business, and God will improve it in his own way and his own time because God, by raising Christ from the dead, has once and for all demonstrated that he ultimately controls the world. He has shown that under his sovereignty evil and death do not have the last word. Christ has the last word. Therefore we can do the work of Christ in the world, assured that though we do not see the results of our labours, our labours are not in vain.

Martin Luther King was a servant of God who refused to succumb to the illusion of futility. He proved it at every step in his struggle to achieve civil rights, even though beating his fists against the iron monster of racism seemed like beating a Russian tank with a rubber-soled running-shoe. He proved it in his acceptance speech of the Nobel Peace Prize at Oslo when he said:

> "I accept this award today with . . . an audacious faith in the future of mankind. I refuse to accept the idea that the 'isness' of man's present nature makes him morally incapable of reaching up for the eternal 'oughtness' that forever confronts him. I refuse to accept the idea that man is mere flotsam and jetsam in a river of life, unable to influence the unfolding events which surround him. I refuse to accept the view that mankind is so tragically bound to the starless midnight of racism and war that the bright daybreak of peace and brotherhood can never become a reality. I refuse to accept the cynical notion that nation after nation must spiral down a militaristic stairway into the hall of thermo-nuclear destruction. I believe that unarmed truth and unconditional love will have the final word in reality."[1]

But Martin Luther King was assassinated, his body destroyed and his career aborted by the very world that he tried to improve. Doesn't that prove that futility is no illusion? Not if God raised Jesus from the dead! Not if Jesus Christ is still the Lord of history! Martin Luther King was a man in Christ, and in Jesus Christ our work for God is never futile.

[1] Quoted in *What Manner of Man* by Lerone Bennett, Jr., Johnson Publishing Company, Inc., New York, 1968, p. 141.

Chapter 9

THE ILLUSION OF HAPPINESS

When we speak of our "culture" we generally mean man's own interpretation of the situation in which he lives. We mean the intellectual and spiritual climate created by schools and universities, by newspapers, television and other media of education and mass communication. We mean the climate into which our children are born, in which they grow up, which conditions their minds, shapes their values and moulds their characters. We are all the products of a culture.

Although we don't intentionally tell lies to our children, it goes without saying that if we bring them up to believe things which are not true, they will not be conditioned to face the realities of life. If the culture contains certain illusions, then our children are in for a rude awakening, because sooner or later these illusions are going to be exploded, perhaps with traumatic effect on their personalities. Life itself will explode some of them without any help from the Bible, although it would be kinder if we saved our children from some of the shocks by teaching them the Bible in their earliest years. Whatever else the Bible does for them, it introduces them to a supremely realistic view of life. It introduces them to the supreme Realist. It explodes the illusions of our culture.

One of the big illusions, which our children are brainwashed to believe, is the illusion of happiness. It is promoted by motion picture producers, song-writers, politicans, parents and even by the Church. It is the vested interest of advertisers and moneylenders who try to convince us with great dignity that we shall never experience real happiness until we have tried a certain deodorant or taken a holiday now on the "pay-later" plan. Not that happiness itself is an illusion. Our children will always be meeting genuinely happy people; they may find happiness themselves, perhaps in circumstances which they never expected. Nevertheless, we ought to set our children free from illusions *about* happiness if we hope to educate them for life; and we have no better way of doing that than by introducing them to Jesus.

It is strange how eager we are to introduce our children to every kind of master except the one person whom the centuries acknowledge to be the Master of Life itself. Jesus may not have been a master of politics or engineering or music. He never constructed a government, a bridge or a symphony but he did construct a life. He knew how to live. He was the one man ever to stand on the stage of history who lived the complete human life for which God has created us. In him personality found its loftiest expression; he made of our life the most splendid thing ever to appear in this world. Therefore, to educate our children for life, without regard to the character and teaching of Jesus, would be no less unfair than educating them in philosophy without regard to Socrates, or in literature without regard to Shakespeare. If we hope to teach our children anything about happiness we certainly owe it to them to tell them what Jesus said and demonstrated about happiness. They will learn that the Master of Life explodes many of our popular illusions.

Jesus explodes the illusion that happiness is the chief end of life. Because many people go through life clinging to that very illusion, it is no wonder that they are anxious to avoid Jesus. No wonder that so many forces in our society align themselves against him, against his Church, his Gospel, his teaching and all that they represent. No wonder that the advertisers and entertainers and popular philosophers, who have a vested interest in extravagance, cupidity and permissiveness, are careful not to mention what Jesus said on those subjects. They teach precisely that happiness is the chief end of life, and Jesus queers their pitch.

The historic Jesus was himself a supremely happy man. We may not always gain that impression from the way that some artists have portrayed him or the way some churches worship him or the way that some Christians try to imitate him. In art, in liturgy and in Christian morals Jesus often appears as a wet blanket, a quencher of happiness; yet nothing could be less faithful to the character of Jesus in the Gospels. In a prison in the southern United States a commercial artist, serving a life sentence, painted a portrait of Jesus which shows the Saviour with a beaming smile. He has made thousands of copies of "The Smiling Christ" and sent them all over the world. He believes that it is an authentic portrayal of the Man of Galilee who was probably the most radiant personality in Palestine, who came upon people like sunshine breaking through the clouds and whose very presence turned sorrow into joy.

Moreover, Jesus wanted other people to be happy. It tore his great loving heart to see so little happiness in the world around him, to see human spirits held down and broken by fear, worry, anxiety, resentment and depression. Jesus came on earth to release people from these gloomy, enslaving moods. He came to offer them life, the full, joyous, satisfying life which he embodied in his own person and which attracted so many of them when they saw it before their eyes. "I am come," he said, "that they might have life and have it abundantly." (John 10:10.) In his teachings he spoke about happiness. He made it the subject of his greatest sermon which begins, "Blessed are the poor in spirit . . . Blessed are they that mourn . . . Blessed are the meek . . .". (Matthew 5:1 ff.) To be sure, "blessedness" has a richer, larger, deeper and more spiritual meaning than "happiness", but blessedness contains happiness just as a red-hot iron contains fire.

Yet it would be wrong to say that Jesus himself was in all places and in all circumstances a happy person, because the Gospels show him in some very different moods. We see him in tears, weeping at the grave of Lazarus, lamenting over the city that was to reject him—"O Jerusalem, Jerusalem . . ." We see him in anger, lashing out against hypocrisy and corruption, calling the Pharisees "whited sepulchres" and overturning the tables of the moneychangers in the temple. We see him in agony, the emotional agony of Gethsemane, the bodily agony of the Cross, the spiritual agony of feeling forsaken by God. Looking at Jesus as the representative Man, the one sent by God to show us the whole range of our human experience on this earth, we see that happiness is meant to be only one side of life. Many of life's experiences do make and ought to make us unhappy.

Jesus wanted men to be happy but never did he deceive them by asking them to believe that happiness is the chief end of life. That would have been a lie, a denial of the whole purpose of his ministry and teaching, because it would have spread the very cancer of selfishness which he came to cure. The pursuit of happiness can be a self-centred pursuit, something that a person seeks only for himself and for which he will pay any price and make other people pay any price. Think of the goals forsaken, the ideals betrayed, the useful careers aborted, the hearts and homes broken by selfish people who gave first priority to their own happiness. Jesus pointed to other priorities. He taught that there are some things in life more important than happiness—fidelity, honour, truth, justice, loyalty, love, sacrifice, the Kingdom of God. He said words to the effect that whoever hoards happiness in a spiritual bank account may wake up one day and find that it has been devalued; whereas he who spends himself in the pursuit of unselfish goals may find that he has unknowingly built up a substantial balance of happiness. If we introduce our children to the teaching and character of Jesus, they will most surely learn from him that happiness is not the chief end of life.

Jesus explodes the illusion that happiness can be found by searching for it. To many people that comes as something of a shock, because they do spend their lives in a never-ending pursuit of happiness. They chase it down one avenue after another—pleasure, sex, marriage, work, drugs, travel, social service and even religion. They are always changing things, always between jobs, or between wives, always on the move from one house, one community, one career or one church to another. They are victims of the big illusion that a simple change of scenery will satisfy their restless desires and give them the feeling of happiness which they have hitherto been denied.

Such people can become as frustrated as a dog chasing its tail. They are never going to catch up with happiness. Always it will elude them like a bubble floating in the air; and if it does come within their grasp it will burst, leaving their hands wet and sticky. There is a very simple reason why happiness cannot be found by searching for it, and that is that we carry the source of our happiness or unhappiness inside us; therefore we take it into each new situation. Happiness is a state of mind; it flows from the inside out, not from the outside in. That is why people have found it in some unusual places. A leader of the Norwegian underground, describing the hardships and dangers of his life during the Nazi occupation, said in a kind of wonderment that one day it came to him that even in this hellish existence he was what men would call a happy man.

Ever since James Hilton wrote his fascinating book, *Lost Horizon*, the name "Shangri-La" has been synonymous with happiness. I read an article written by a camera technician who went with a film company to make a picture in the Himalayas at the place reputed to be the fabled, ever-happy, heaven-on-earth, Shangri-La. He was shocked by what he found—a valley full of barren rocks and scrub growth and lean children dressed in rags. They ran to meet the visitors bearing bowls of flowers and ushered them to the palace of the Mir which was a simple building like a farmhouse. The Mir proudly showed them his two prize possessions, symbols of his power: a telephone that wouldn't work and a piano so badly out of tune that it couldn't be played. Such poverty was a far cry from the paradise portrayed by James Hilton. The camera technician said that he felt dreadfully let down until suddenly he woke up to one thing about these people—they were happy. In all Shangri-La he saw not a single worried face; he saw many faces wrinkled with smiles. So, on the door of his own farmhouse back in America he placed a sign that read, "Shangri-La". When someone asks him about it, he tells the story of his visit to the fabled, rocky heaven-on-earth and of the lesson he learned there: Shangri-La is a state of mind.[1]

Happiness cannot be found by searching for it, because the search is so often self-defeating. The very act of trying to be happy is a selfish act which puts us in a frame of mind where happiness becomes impossible. In a book written some years ago, Ernest Freemont Tittle suggested that the moment we give first priority to our own happiness, inevitably we begin to play safe, and before long we are playing entirely too safe to be happy. We stop working at the point where we can get easy pleasure out of our work, and so deprive ourselves of the greater pleasure that comes from hard work. We stop giving at a point where we can give without very much cost, and so deprive ourselves of the joy that comes from giving which has reached the point of sacrifice. We even stop loving where it begins to hurt, and so miss the supreme joy of a love that "suffers long and is kind". Thus the pursuit of happiness is often an unhappy pursuit because it engenders in the pursuer a self-concern. It defeats its own object. In our over-anxiety to be happy we stop at the very point where we have our first great chance to be happy.

Albert Schweitzer wrote: "One thing I know. The only ones among you who will be really happy are the ones who have sought and found how to serve." Schweitzer, who spoke from experience, was saying that happiness must never be sought for its own sake; it can be found only as the by-product of a search for something more important. That was Jesus' teaching, especially in the Beatitudes. (Matthew 5:1 ff.) "Let me tell you," he said, "who the blessed, the truly happy people are"; and he gives us a strange list, so completely

[1] Published in *Guideposts*, August, 1959, p. 8.

contrary to our ideas of happiness that we can scarcely believe it. Here are the happy people: the poor in spirit who stand before God claiming nothing for themselves; the mourners whose sympathy for human sorrow has saddened their spirits; the meek who have learned to control their strength; the righteous who seek for goodness as for food and drink; the merciful who live with their brethren in charity; the pure in heart who are utterly sincere; the peacemakers whose lives are dedicated to the promotion of peace; the sufferers who have learned to suffer for the right. Plainly Jesus is saying that we shall find happiness not by searching for it but rather as the by-product of a search for something more important. That's what our children learn when we introduce them to Jesus.

Jesus explodes the illusion that a man can find happiness without God in his life. There is a puzzling encounter in the eleventh chapter of Luke's Gospel. A woman in the crowd called out to Jesus, "Happy is the womb that carried you and the breasts that suckled you." Jesus rejoined, "No, happy are those who hear the word of God and keep it." Why did he answer her in that way? Hers was a womanly reaction. A mother herself perhaps, she was simply marvelling at the wisdom and power and popularity of Jesus and saying, in effect, "Your mother must be proud of you. You must make her very happy." We don't know the tone of voice in which Jesus replied but we can be sure that it was not a discourteous tone. He must have smiled as he gently told the woman that it is an illusion to think that such things as parental pride can in themselves produce happiness. He was saying that it is a mistake to expect happiness from any relationship that the world can give us. The happy man is the man who stands in a relationship of obedience to God. Only God can give us lasting happiness.

If Jesus spoke the truth he provides an insight into the reason for many unhappy marriages. Someone will say after a couple have separated, "I can't understand what went wrong. Theirs was a perfect marriage." Yes, but what makes a perfect marriage? Physical compatibility? Similar backgrounds? Common interests? Planned parenthood? Mortgage-free house? Congenial in-laws? If these things alone guaranteed a happy home, we should not need to relax the divorce laws, and the civil courts would not now be glutted with applications for divorces. It is not by accident that we begin the Marriage Service by quoting the words of a Hebrew psalmist: "Except the Lord build the house, they labour in vain that build it." Many marriages break down because they are do-it-yourself jobs; they are cannibalistic, feeding off their own flesh and lacking the spiritual resources which only God can give and which God does give when the love of man and woman is consciously lifted up and perfected in his inseparable love.

Jesus taught that truth in his Parable of the Big Feast (Luke 14:15 ff.) which, even as a lesson in social discourtesy, has strikingly modern overtones. The occasion was a dinner-party to which the "best people" of the community had been invited. When all things were ready, the host, according to the custom of the time, dispatched a messenger to summon the guests who had formally accepted his original invitation. The messenger returned to say that without exception the guests had reneged on their promise to come, offering excuses which were neither sincere nor substantial. The host felt insulted. "All right!" he exploded. "We don't need them! Let them stay away! Don't admit them even if they show up! We'll have a party without them!" Three of the excuses are specified. The first guest said, "I have bought a piece of ground, and I must needs go and see it"—which in our idiom means that he had made a capital investment of money and that it took priority over his invitation to the Kingdom of God. The second offered the excuse, "I have bought five yoke of oxen, and I go to prove them"—which in our idiom means that he had acquired a new labour-saving device and that his work was more important to him than the Kingdom Banquet. The third offered no excuse. He simply said that he had just been married and set up a home and therefore couldn't attend the party. (Maybe his wife wouldn't let him out.) Money, work, home—the elemental factors of social life which should and can produce happiness if we accept them as gifts from God, meeting-places with God, means of serving God. Sought and worshipped for their own sake, however, and allowed to stand between us and God, our money, our work and our homes may become not a blessing but a curse and may shut us out from the happiness which God alone can give.

In terms of worldly satisfactions Jesus had no right to be happy. Piecing together the bits of his biography in the Gospels, we see that he was born in a rented stable in an occupied country and that right away his earthly parents became refugees. Returning to their village, they brought him up in a peasant's cottage, apprenticed him as a common craftsman and did very little to help him when he left home and began his public ministry. He never married, he lived in poverty, he was opposed by his enemies, betrayed and deserted by his friends and in the end executed like a common criminal. Yet on the very eve of his execution Jesus spoke to his disciples not of sadness but of happiness. He said, "These things have I spoken unto you, that my joy may be in you, and that your joy may be full." (John 15:11.) We can only conclude that either he had gone mad or else that he spoke the truth when he said to the woman in the crowd, "Happy are they that hear the word of God and keep it." Jesus had heard the word of God, a word directing him along the lonely road of sacrificial love. Jesus obeyed that word and in his obedience he found a happiness that the world cannot give or take away.

So let's stop fooling our children. Let's stop filling their minds with illusions about happiness. Let's tell them the truth and condition them to meet life as we teach them that some things in life are more important than happiness, that happiness can be found only as the by-product of a search for something more important, and that God alone can give them true happiness in the measure that they hear his Word and keep it. Let's introduce our children to Jesus.

CHAPTER 10

THE ILLUSION OF FAILURE

The middle-aged man squirmed uncomfortably on the psychiatrist's couch. He had been under treatment for several months. For the umpteenth time he diagnosed his own illness. "I know my trouble, doctor," he said. "I'm a failure and I just can't take it." It was true that he felt an acute sense of failure. He had put everything that he had into a new job and had failed to make a go of it. Nobody held it against him, but he held it against himself, he worried himself sick. The psychiatrist was a man of few words. Most of the time he sat in a chair writing, asking an occasional question and generally letting the patient think through his own situation. He was becoming bored, however, by the monotonous litany, "I am a failure." One day he said gently to the patient, "Look! What you've *done* and what you *are* are two different things. Sure you've failed, but that doesn't mean that you are a failure."

The patient was a casualty of our culture which is shot through with illusions, among them the illusion that to fail in something automatically makes a man a failure. From his earliest years his parents, who had never "made it" themselves, pounded his conscience with the big lie that he must succeed and that if he didn't succeed he would be a failure. At school his teachers brandished the big stick of examinations over his head and brainwashed him to believe that if he didn't pass them he would be a failure. Out in the business world he found himself in a climate where men who did not burn incense before the great god of success were branded failures; and having failed to gain the favour of that god, he had now branded himself a failure and become an emotional wreck.

Any intelligent person will agree that the purpose of education is not only to impart factual knowledge but to prepare our children for life, to condition their minds so that they will be able to deal constructively with every experience and eventuality. Surely, then, it would be the mark of wisdom and kindness to prepare them for non-success. Somewhere along the way we ought to teach them that what the world calls failure is an integral element of life, that they are not expected to succeed in everything they do and that in all of life's testing experiences—school exams, business careers, marriage, parenthood, friendship and moral ideals—they run the risk of having to say "I have failed!" It is also the mark of wisdom and kindness, however, to teach our children that what they *do* and what they *are* are two different things. To say "I have failed" does not give a person the right to say "I am a failure".

At this point we can learn a valuable lesson from the Apostle Paul, a gifted, versatile, dynamic man who unquestionably succeeded in many things which he undertook. Yet in one of his New Testament letters he makes a candid confession of failure. In the third chapter of his Letter to the Philippians he writes words which have been translated, "Brethren, I do not count myself to have succeeded." (3:13.) They cannot be translated, "I count myself to be a failure." That would have been a character-judgment which Paul would never have presumed to make because he was too much of a realist. A man may be competent to judge his own actions but he is not competent to judge his own character. He is certainly not competent to call himself a failure, because even the action of failure, as the world defines it, is often an illusion and is seen to be such when we take account of certain facts.

In the first place, *success and failure can be measured only by our own goals.* We have to be very clear what we are trying to do before we decide whether we have succeeded or failed. One critic wrote of an opera singer, "She works hard along the line of least resistance. She always succeeds because she never attempts difficult roles." Any person can succeed provided he never attempts anything difficult and always chooses goals that are easily within his grasp. The skier who reaches the bottom of the beginners' hill in an upright position can shout proudly, "Look at me! I'm a success!" Suppose he tries a steeper slope and falls flat on his face half-way down. Does that mean that he is a failure?

It is here that some of us quarrel with our systems of education which up to now have placed so much stock in success and so little in sheer effort. We persist in measuring students against other students and not against their own goals. We award university scholarships on the basis of academic brilliance, which is manifestly unfair, because some students are so naturally endowed with brilliance that they can learn almost without effort. If they simply propped books up against their heads they would absorb the contents by a process of osmosis. What of the student, far below scholarship level, who nevertheless works hard during his school career and makes a steady progress towards goals which for him are demanding and difficult? Let's give that student a free place in university, because he has qualities which will enrich and elevate society, qualities to be recognized and rewarded rather than stifled by unfair competition.

We are told that once it was the custom in India for a university student, who had failed to pass his examinations, to carry a card with his name followed by the letters, "B.A.—failed". One admires this gallant gesture, this frank admission of non-success. Behind it is the philosophy that a man ought to be judged not only by his achievements but by the goals towards which he has worked, even though he has failed to reach those goals, because presumably he is of greater value to society than if he had never tried to reach them in the first place. Paul Tillich wrote, "He who risks and fails can be forgiven. He who never risks and never fails is a failure in his whole being." There is more dignity in costly failure than in cheap success.

Not only dignity but satisfaction. Who, after all, gets a greater thrill out of the winter sports—the skier who confines himself to the children's slopes or the more daring person who goes up the chair-lift and joins the men? Who derives a larger sense of fulfilment from his career—the scientist who is satisfied to be a laboratory technician or the research worker who devotes years of patient effort to experiments that may benefit mankind? Who feels himself more useful to society—the social worker whose labours yield a quick and easy harvest or the great reformer who plants the seeds of justice for future generations to reap? Who feels a keener sense of exhilaration—the decent man who simply stays out of prison or the idealist who measures himself by the moral wisdom of the ages? Robert Browning believed that "a man's reach should exceed his grasp, or what's a heaven for?" It is one of his favourite themes that life finds its richest fulfilment not in success but in striving:

> "That low man seeks a little thing to do,
> Sees it and does it;
> This high man with a great thing to pursue
> Dies ere he knows it."

Thus a man may set his feet on a path that leads inevitably to non-success. He may choose goals so challenging, so exalted and so difficult that he never expects to reach them within his own lifetime. Does that make him a failure? "Brethren," wrote Paul, "I do not count myself to have succeeded." But we have to ask, "Not succeeded in what?" In the preceding verses Paul tells us: "All I care for is to know Christ, to experience the power of his resurrection, and to share his sufferings, in growing conformity with his death, if only I may finally arrive at the resurrection from the dead." Paul is saying that he wants to identify himself completely with Jesus Christ. He wants to do nothing less than reproduce in his life the character and experience of Jesus. To that he aspired in that he felt that he had not succeeded. How could he feel otherwise? How can any man succeed in reaching such an exalted goal? Yet these are the goals that give meaning to life, and as long as we strive towards them, it is an illusion to think that we are failures.

We can go a step further and say that *failure is an illusion until it has stood the test of time*. Life itself validates that truth, as every educator knows from experience. The wise teacher never judges a child on the basis of present achievement because he knows that the child who lacks lustre today may shine most brilliantly tomorrow. It would be cruel, therefore, and dishonest to tell him that he is a failure. Indeed, time can make nonsense of our hasty judgments, as two college administrators agreed when they exchanged views on the wisdom of expelling students. One of them said, "I only once expelled a man. He seemed quite a hopeless case—skipped lectures, failed examinations, had no self-discipline, was constantly getting into trouble. I put him down as a total failure." "Where is he now?" asked the other administrator. The reply came rather sheepishly, "He is now the president of a much larger university than this one."

Only in retrospect can a human career be judged a success or a failure. The Christian minister knows from experience that a man who does God's work must learn the lesson imparted by the psychiatrist to his patient, or he himself may end up on a psychiatrist's couch. "Success" and "failure" are two words which ought to have no place in a minister's vocabulary for the very reason that he is engaged in a work where any but the most superficial results are rarely obvious to him. Many a minister, his spirit broken by a sense of dismal failure, might pass a different verdict if he could look back and see his career from the vantage-point of eternity. Canon Twells, the writer of the beautiful hymn, "At even 'ere the sun was set", tells about a friend of his, a layman to whom a great preacher of his day confessed sadly, "If I ever turned one heart from the ways of disobedience to the wisdom of the just, God has withheld the assurance from me." In that sense of failure the preacher died. At the funeral the layman noticed by the graveside a stranger who seemed deeply grieved and he asked, "You knew him, I suppose?" The stranger replied, "Knew him? No, I never spoke to him; but I owe to him my soul."

Reading the great biographies of the world, we can see that all the towering figures in history were thwarted by frustrations and defeats to a point where they felt tempted to quit and write themselves off as failures. How much poorer our common life would be if the men who have most enriched it had done exactly that! Their very greatness stemmed from the fact that they did not pass judgment on themselves. They took the larger and more realistic view that failure is an illusion until it has stood the test of time and that no enterprise can be judged a success or failure on the day that it happens; it cannot be so judged until all the days are in and the total added up.

What finer example than Abraham Lincoln whose career up to a certain point seemed a sorry succession of failures! As a young man he went to the Black Hawk War a captain and, through no fault of his own, returned a private. That brought to an end his military career. Then his little shop in a country village "winked out", as he used to say, marking his failure as a business man. As a lawyer in Springfield, Illinois, he was too impractical, too unpolished, too temperamental to be a success. Turning to politics, he was defeated in his first campaign for the Legislature, defeated in his first attempt to be nominated for Congress, defeated in his application to be Commissioner of the General Land Office, defeated in the Senatorial Election of 1854, defeated in his efforts for the Vice-Presidency in 1856, defeated again in the Senatorial election of 1858. Yet 1861 found him in the White House as President of the United States. Refusing to accept his frustrations and failures as final, Lincoln persisted with a dogged determination that culminated in overwhelming success.

Seen in that light, an experience of failure may be one of

life's creative experiences. It may be the best thing that can happen to us, teaching us lessons that we can learn in no other way. Some of us need to fail in order to be jolted out of easy complacency and compelled to work and struggle so that we can achieve our true potential. There was a modern saint who gave thanks to God in these words: "Thou hast broken my dreams, but only that I might learn to think in Thy broad day. Thou hast put aside my plans, but only that I might open my eyes to the depth and clearness of Thy plan for me." Think it possible that God in his superior wisdom may even cause us to fail sometimes in order that we abandon our mediocre purposes and be driven to discover his great purpose for our lives. Something like that had happened to Paul who said, in effect, "All right, I have failed to be a Christ-like Christian, but that's over and done with now. So let's forget past failure and not talk about it any more." Then, having buried the past, Paul set his face steadfastly towards the future: "This one thing I do . . . I press on to grasp the purpose for which Christ has grasped me." When a man says *that*, it's an illusion to believe that he is a failure.

Failure can never be anything but an illusion until we establish the criterion of success. What, in fact, are the criteria popularly accepted in our culture? Who may be called a successful man in terms of the values and standards of the world? Obviously the man who has made money, who lives in the big house and drives two cars and buys his wife a mink coat and takes his family on expensive holidays. Or he may be the V.I.P. who has made a name for himself as a scholar, an author, an athlete, a musician or a scientist. Or he may be the big boss in business, industry, labour, politics, the army or even the Church. These are the idols whom we hold up before our children from their very earliest years, the men who have "arrived". And their success is very real; it is no illusion.

The illusion creeps in when we hold up their achievements in money, fame and status as the sole criterion of success. It is an illusion to believe that a man who "makes it" in one area of life is automatically a success in terms of life itself. If we are going to be realistic we shall recognize that what the world calls success need not always be an index of a man's character or his expertise. A respected Hollywood actor wrote honestly, "There is an ingredient in success which goes beyond effort, even beyond talent—an element of luck, of knowing the right person, of being in the right place at the right time, of simple, gratuitous fate." Moreover, we all know people who have been very lucky in their contacts and opportunities, who have climbed the ladder of material and professional success almost without effort, yet who in terms of their total relationships are lamentable failures. Conversely, we know people who have never achieved wealth and prestige, yet who lead rich and happy lives. It would be a lie to call them failures.

Some years ago I watched a television play called *The Failure*. It was the story of a man who held a minor position in a bank. He did not resent his ordinary status but worked hard and found a sense of fulfilment in his work. His family, however, felt the pinch of his limited income, and his children were plainly embarrassed by it; they envied their friends whose parents could afford to provide them with many luxuries. One day this man overheard his teenage daughter complaining to her mother, "Dad is a failure, isn't he?" But was he a failure—this man who treated his wife with tender fidelity, who did his humble work with diligence and integrity, who was willing to miss the possibility of a promotion so that he could be present at his daughter's graduation from school? As the play progressed, you began to feel that some day his children would look back and be proud of him for providing them with blessings, with values and with a love that no money can buy. Though he had failed to make a substantial living, you got the impression that he had succeeded phenomenally in making a life. Low in his credit-rating, yet as a husband, a father, an employee and as a man, he rated highly indeed.

No wonder the hippies protest against the values of our bourgeois culture! No wonder they reject the world's standards of success. Who, after all, is qualified to appraise the success or failure of any human life? In this world there are at least two points of view, the human and the Divine; and if we read the New Testament and come to terms with the Divine viewpoint revealed in Jesus we shall find that the failure which God accepts is often more significant than the success which the world admires. Perhaps God has a special place in his heart for those whom the world judges and who judge themselves to be failures. That thought has been expressed in a beautiful poem:

"God has a special place for still-born things,
The things that never were and should have been:
The little songs no singer ever sings,
The beauty of a picture hung unseen,
A noble heart that loved with no return,
And deeds well meant which somehow turned out ill,
A lovely flame that vainly tried to burn
But could not last, though all the winds were still,
The early flower that no-one ever sees
Making its way through ground iced hard with sleet,
A Caesar to whom no man bends his knees,

The Christ-like smile that meets each fresh defeat:
God treats them very tenderly for He
Knows what the pain of stifled things can be."[1]

"Brethren," wrote Paul, "I do not count myself to have succeeded." Behind this confession lies the conviction that sometimes the greatest gift a man can offer to God is the gift of failure. That does not mean that the man himself is a failure; else Jesus is a failure because Jesus was crucified, and in the eyes of the world the Cross appears as history's most colossal failure. But the Cross was God's success. It was God's plan whereby every man who identifies himself with the obedience of Christ can share in the victory of Christ. That means that God meets us in our failures. It means that failure can be a Sacrament. It means also that what the world calls failure can be an illusion.

[1] "A Special Place" by Dorothy Quick, published in *Changing Winds*, copyright 1935 by Dorothy Quick. G. P. Putnam's Sons, New York, Publishers. Used by permission.

CHAPTER 11

THE ILLUSION OF FREEDOM

July 2nd, 1968 was an important date in Canadian history. On that day the new Parliamentary Bill on Divorce became law, and the next day the civil clerks buttressed themselves for the deluge. Before the month was over, the Province of Ontario alone received 650 applications for divorces as compared with 200 during the same month in 1967. Hitherto the main ground for divorce in Canada had to be an allegation of adultery, but now the basis had been broadened to include such ambiguous grounds as mental cruelty and marriage breakdown. Though the new laws are more honest and humane than the old, they are also frightening. It is feared that when marriages can be dissolved easily, there will not be the compulsion to make marriage work, and inevitably this poses a threat to the permanence and stability of the home.

The Canadian Government did not act arbitrarily. Like every democratic government it took a clear sounding of public opinion and acceded to the wishes of the majority of citizens. No government that hopes to stay in office will attempt a policy for which the electors do not have a conscience. Politics reflect a nation's character, and people usually get the legislation they want. In this instance, as in the proposed new laws dealing with abortion and homosexuality, the Canadian people have plainly indicated that they want a larger measure of personal freedom.

The desire for freedom, even to a point of permissiveness, has become a prevailing characteristic of our culture. The original draft of one of the reports of the World Council of Churches Assembly in Sweden contained the following sentences: "Modern methods of preventing conception raise the question in the minds of many, both young and not so young, whether sleeping together may someday become as ordinary as eating together. This is a challenge to our Christian teaching about chastity." That somewhat earthy language was later toned down, but the sense of it remained. Today all the old Christian standards, not only with regard to sex relations but with regard to all forms of human behaviour, are being challenged, and the challenge comes from the spokesmen of our culture—the novelists, the motion picture producers, the script writers, the free-lance broadcasters and even some theologians. They are asking, "Can any rules of behaviour possibly cover all the varied and complex situations in which men and women find themselves? Is man intended to be fenced in by the old moral laws? Is he not rather intended to be free and to decide for himself what is the moral thing to do in every situation?"

It would seem that we have a new patron saint in our culture—the Prodigal Son. We have looked upon him as an individual type, but there is also a general sense in which he represents our generation. He wanted to be free, and that was the overruling impulse that drove him to demand of his father, "Give me my share of the property." (Luke 15:12, *N.E.B.*). Evidently he felt inhibited and held down by his parents and by his elder brother who later showed himself to be something of a prude. The younger boy wanted to cut loose from the restricting rules of his childhood home. He wanted to be able to come down to breakfast in the mornings without having to answer the nagging question, "Where were you last night?" He wanted to be free.

So, he was given his freedom and released from his mother's apron strings, though the parable makes no mention of his mother. He took his share of the property, which he quickly sold, and emigrated to a far country where he could live on his own terms and be his own master without having to answer to anyone. He was free! But was he? In the far country the Prodigal Son made the astonishing discovery that freedom is an illusion. He learned by bitter experience that no man ever escapes from bondage; he simply exchanges one bondage for another. Wherever he goes his life is hedged by restrictions. Always he is the slave of somebody or something. Considered in that light, the Parable of the Prodigal Son becomes a sharp sword that punctures the illusion of freedom.

It shows us that *no man is free from the restrictions imposed on him by his own personality*. One sentence: "A few days later the younger son turned the whole of his share into cash and left home for a distant country, where he squandered it in reckless living"; one sentence, but it speaks volumes about the young man's personality. Presumably he might not have squandered his money in reckless living. Many a man, turned loose on his own and given sufficient capital, has emigrated to another city or country and made a fortune. Not so the Prodigal; he didn't have the strength of character; he was the slave of his own weakness.

It can happen to anybody. Every human character has weaknesses which show themselves when certain childhood restrictions are removed. Suppose we continue to relax the liquor laws and lower the public drinking age to 18, giving our young people the freedom to which the liquor interests claim that they are entitled? Cold statistics show that one in every fifteen new drinkers will find his freedom an illusion because he will simply exchange the bondage of the law for the bondage of his own weakness. For him liquor will not be a luxury but a necessity. He may not want to drink all the time but he will discover that he has no choice. He is a compulsive drinker. Alcohol will be as essential to him as insulin is to a diabetic. He may hate the taste of the whisky which he craves. He may hate himself for the hurt that his drinking does to his family and his own career but he cannot control it. The habit has him hooked. He is not free not to drink. His bottle is a ball and chain. He is the slave of his own weakness.

Think of the emotions that hold the human personality in bondage. We can almost visualize some of them as demons hovering around the delivery room at a hospital and fighting for control of the baby about to be born. *Ambition* says, "Let me at him first. His parents feel frustrated by their own failures, so they will try to achieve success through their son. I'll make that boy so obsessed with getting ahead that one big failure will turn him into a neurotic." *Jealousy* says, "Let me take him. He's going to be an only child. I'll see that his parents spoil him so that he goes through all of life as a selfish, egotistical, possessive brat." *Insecurity* chimes in, "No, he belongs to me. His parents don't really want him, so they won't give him much love. They don't have too much love for each other. I'll make him so emotionally disturbed that he will never be capable of constructive achievements or right relationships." *Hostility* says, "Then he's a natural for me. Let me sow the seeds of suspicion, prejudice and hatred in his mind. That ought to make him a hell-raiser." So all these demons get their hooks into the soul of the foetus, and even if he lives a hundred years, they will never let him go. Long before he asserts his youthful independence and begins to cut loose from external restraints this boy will be a slave to the weakness of his own personality.

People who nurse the illusion of freedom may try to claim support from the Apostle Paul who wrote a great deal about personal freedom. Some of us might have been spared unhealthy guilt feelings if when we were teenagers we had read and digested these two-fisted statements from Paul's Letter to the Colossians:

> "Why let other people dictate to you: 'Do not handle this, do not taste that, and do not touch the other'—all of them things that must perish as soon as they are used? That is to follow merely human injunctions and teaching. True, it has an air of wisdom, with its forced piety, its self-mortification, and its severity to the body; but it is of no use at all in combating sensuality." (Colossians 2:20–23, *N.E.B.*)

So the Christian is free from external rules and from the self-styled dictators of human conduct, but does that make him a free man? Not according to Paul. He knows that there is a stronger bondage which even a Christian cannot escape—the bondage of his own impulses, his own actions and reactions, which he cannot control but which control him. Pointing to himself, Paul confesses,

> "I do not understand my own actions. For I do not do what I want, but I do the very thing I hate . . . I find it to be a law that when I want to do right, evil lies close at hand.

For I delight in the law of God, in my inmost self, but I see in my members another law at war with the law of my mind and making me captive to the law of sin . . ." (Romans 7:15, 21–23, *R.S.V.*)

This inner bondage to his own weakness Paul compared to a corpse strapped on his back and he cried out, "Wretched man that I am! Who will deliver me from this body of death?" Paul discovered that Christ could deliver him but he did not fool himself by nursing the illusion that apart from Christ there is any real freedom.

The Parable of the Prodigal Son shows us that *no man is free from the restrictions imposed on him by other people.* The story continues, again packing a wealth of detail into a few short sentences: "He had spent it all, when a severe famine fell upon that country and he began to feel the pinch. So he went and attached himself to one of the local landowners, who sent him on to his farm to mind the pigs. He would have been glad to fill his belly with the pods that the pigs were eating; and no one gave him anything." What a terrible indignity for the young Jew—forced to mind pigs and share their slops! It would never have happened at home among his father and friends. The point is, however, that he was not at home among his father and friends. He was out in society among strangers where he discovered that they also exercised restrictions upon him, restrictions more distasteful than any he had ever chafed under at home. Released from parental authority, the Prodigal found that he had simply exchanged a benevolent bondage for a harsh one.

Look at these three factors—the famine, the landowner and the hard-hearted people. They represent the very factors in society which always inhibit personal freedom. The famine represents our social interrelatedness. It was a catastrophe of nature, but politics and economics were bound up in it to the extent that it might possibly have been averted. Joseph in Egypt saw the signs of famine and persuaded the Pharaoh to appoint him as the director of a programme of food conservation which later became a programme of economic assistance and thereby saved other nations from starvation. No one, apparently, foresaw the famine that struck the country to which the Prodigal had emigrated, with the result that no one escaped it. In that sense social catastrophe, be it famine, depression, revolution or war, is always a tyrant; it enslaves everybody, and no one escapes. The World Council of Churches may give its blessing to conscientious Christians who object to participating in "a particular war" but even the World Council cannot save them from participating in wars, because war in today's world is a social catastrophe which in some way involves all of us whether we oppose it or not. Freedom may be real on a desert island; in society it is an illusion.

The landowner in the parable represents the law. As an employer he had a right to send his hired man into the piggery, and as an employee the Prodigal had no choice but to obey. He learned what Victor Hugo called the great lesson of the French Revolution, viz., that "the liberty of one citizen ends where the liberty of another citizen begins". That principle is basic to any ordered and responsible society; it is the foundation of law, the law which restricts you and at the same time protects you by restricting your neighbour. Mr. Bumble said that "the law is an ass!", but that makes the ass the king of the beasts, because men certainly behave like beasts, with less intelligence than donkeys, when there is no law to restrict them. The alternatives are not law or freedom but bondage to law or bondage to chaos.

Inversely, the hard-hearted people in the parable represent the restraints of love. The Prodigal needed their charity, even though they didn't give it to him, and to that extent he was not free from them. In that sense none of us is free from other people. We are in bondage to them because we need their love and because their love sets us free from a very different kind of bondage. In childhood the love of parents saves us from bondage to hunger, homelessness, hostility and lifelong insecurity. In marriage the love of husband or wife sets us free from bondage to lust, loneliness, frustration and self-centredness. Silas Marner in George Eliot's novel was a mean, miserable miser. In his wealth he thought that he was free from people, but he was not free from the thief who stole his money, not free from the foundling child who loved him and whose love turned him from a miser into a man. We are never free from other people. Even their opinions and our desire for their friendship and respect exercise a restraining influence on our conduct. "What will people think?" we ask. In one way or another we are in bondage. So we had better make up our minds that personal freedom is an illusion.

The Parable of the Prodigal Son shows us that *no man can be free from the restrictions imposed on him by God.* When the foolish boy sank low enough to see what a mess he had made of his life "he came to his senses", or as the older translation puts it, "he came to himself", his true self—not the degraded rebel but the beloved son who had lived with dignity and honour in his father's home. In a tremendous victory over his pride he made up his mind to return home, prepared to grovel, if necessary, to accept the status of a hired servant in his father's household. But that was not necessary. His father, who had been watching for him daily, saw him in the distance and rushed down the road to meet him, smothered his contrition with an outburst of love and received him back to his home and heart as one returned from the dead.

The point of the parable is that the Prodigal never did get away from his father. He broke loose from his father's authority but he found that he could never break loose from his father's love. Everything reminded him of it. He saw it by contrast in the despotism of the landowner, the callousness of the citizens, the degrading nature of his work, the aching hunger of his stomach, and he cried out, "How many of my father's paid servants have more food than they can eat, and here am I, starving to death!" The message comes across loud and clear when we understand that Jesus intends the forgiving father in the parable to represent God. It is a true picture of the God who revealed himself in Jesus, who came where we are, stood by us in our shame and refused to leave us even when we hounded him to a terrible death on a Cross. This God loves us and he never stops loving us. His love is sovereign. It may be a sovereignty on the left hand and it may appear to us as judgment but it is love none the less, and we are never free from it.

That is why the biggest lie being circulated these days is the silly notion that because people no longer believe in a God "out there", neither will they be restricted by moral rules like the Ten Commandments which derive their authority from a God "out there". Disregarding the obvious fact that the Ten Commandments have stood the test of time and have been written into every law code in the civilized world, suppose we set aside the image of God as a King in the sky who punishes us if we disobey his laws. Suppose we think of God as a Loving Father, not outside the world's life but within the world's life, and suppose we think of his love as a principle running through the world's life, is any man free to violate that principle without throwing the world's life into chaos? Is he free to cheat and steal and lie without disrupting the total scheme of things? Is he free to exploit another's personality without damaging his own personality? Is he free to murder another's body or spirit without murdering himself? Someone may argue that these are only the inexorable human consequences of our actions, but what makes these consequences inexorable if not the sovereign love of God? God is not a killjoy or a tyrant or a fool. His rules do not insult our freedom or contradict our common sense. They provide the only framework in which we can live a sane, secure, civilized and satisfying life. Therefore we are not free from them.

The Prodigal Son really came to his senses. He really stumbled on the truth when he admitted to himself that life on any terms with his father offered him more freedom than life on any terms in the far country. Sometimes people reject the Christian religion because it seems too negative and restrictive; it seems to be saying *No* to everything they want to do. What they don't understand is that Christianity never says *No* except as the reflection of a higher *Yes*. Christianity's big business is not to teach us to say *No* to evil but to teach us to say *Yes* to Jesus Christ and in that higher bondage to find freedom from the evils which might otherwise enslave us. Augustine defined freedom as "the blessed compulsion not to do evil, the blessed necessity of not sinning". Jesus said, "Every one who commits sin is a slave of sin . . . if the Son makes you free, you will be free indeed." (John 8:34, 36, *R.S.V.*) Paul called himself "the slave of Christ". In a world where men knew the meaning of slavery and where a slave belonged body and soul to his master Paul used that figure to show how completely he had surrendered himself to the service of Christ and in that higher bondage found perfect freedom.

As a young man, presumably under 30, the Prodigal Son speaks to every young man or woman who chafes under the restrictions of home, school and society and longs to be free to live his own life. That person needs to be told that you can never live your own life. Freedom is an illusion. Always you will be in some kind of bondage. The question is, What bondage? In the fifteenth century Ignatius Loyola, a young soldier, gay, worldly and godless, debarred from further fighting by wounds suffered in battle, came to a monastery, laid his sword upon the altar and placed himself under obedience to Jesus Christ. From that day onwards Loyola found a freedom that he had never known before, a freedom in which all his latent powers grew and developed like a flower coming into full bloom. Every man finds freedom to achieve the highest purpose for his life when he stops fighting and lays down his sword and pledges himself in obedience to the Strong Son of God.

CHAPTER 12

THE ILLUSION OF RELIGION

There is a story told about the head of an Oxford college who was going down the escalator in a London Underground station. It can be a diverting journey, especially for the male of the species, because he can furtively feast his eyes on a series of alluring posters that mainly advertise intimate wearing apparel. One of them read, "For women. For uplift. For general support." Not being as other men are, the college head exclaimed to himself, "Ah! This must be an advertisement for the Church."

"For women. For uplift. For general support." It is exactly the image which many outsiders do have of the Church. They see the Church as a society of neurotic women, of both sexes, whose sagging morale needs uplift and general support. They think that Church people cannot possibly be "whole" persons, else their lives would be self-sufficient and filled with all sorts of interesting things, and they would not have to compensate by turning to religion. It is one of the great illusions of our culture that religion is really nothing more than a refuge for the incompetent and a shelter for the inadequate, a crutch for lame ducks and a spiritual soporific to deaden the shocks of life and make us more comfortable.

Church people themselves sometimes labour under that

illusion. There was an old-fashioned and out-spoken pastor who aspired to be more than a trouble-shooter in his congregation and who regularly and systematically visited his members in their homes. He believed that God can use people when they are physically and morally upright and he wanted to talk to them about it. Usually he notified them by postcard ahead of time and asked that they let him know if they did not plan to be at home. But some folk are not interested in this routine pastoral relationship. One of them telephoned the church secretary and said jauntily, "Tell the minister not to bother visiting us. We'll call him when we need him." The minister was nettled by this rebuff. "And when will they need me?" he exploded. "When something goes wrong! When they are sick or dying or bereaved! When the marriage breaks down or the man loses his job or one of the children gets into trouble! When their laughter turns to tears!" *That's* the big illusion about religion—that it has no place in times of laughter; it becomes relevant only in time of tears.

On all sides these days the *avant-garde* theologians are telling us that we must revise our image of God. It may be just as important that we revise our image of religion. Surely the time has come when the Church, if it would regain the world's respect, must shatter some of the illusions about religion not only in the minds of outsiders but in the minds of Church people themselves. To do so we need to look more closely at the Bible, especially the teachings and ministry of Jesus. Some significant truths emerge.

First, we notice that *the purpose of religion is not only to bring us through the crises but to help us with the duties and relationships of routine living.*

Now that thrift has become economic heresy, you rarely

find people saving up their money for a rainy day, but some still try to do it with their religion. They stuff God away in a bottom drawer and purposely forget his existence while they remain secure in the comforting thought that God will be there if and when they need him. When crisis comes, when sickness strikes, when trouble threatens, and they are frankly frightened, they suddenly remember their spiritual nest-egg and, rushing to that bottom drawer, they pull it open, expecting to find the means of their deliverance. They may find an empty space instead. G. K. Chesterton said that as a young man he put his religious beliefs away in a drawer, and, when he went to look for them, they were not there. The lesson is plain. Religion, if we do not make it the normal habit of our lives, cannot be extemporized in a disaster.

Our culture reflects the illusion of religion. We see it in plays and novels. When the plot reaches a crisis, and the storm is fierce, and the moment tense beyond relief, some scared or pious character in the story announces that things are pretty bad and that they had better pray. Shakespeare in *The Tempest* makes his sailors cry in peril of the storm, "All is lost! To prayers! To prayers! All is lost!" That is the illusion—that God is a crisis measure, prayer a neon-marked emergency exit, and that religion is meant only to undergird us and pull us through in times of stress.

Let it be thankfully acknowledged that a strong religious faith does avail mightily in the crises of life. John G. Paton, the great missionary to the New Hebrides, who had to bury his young wife with his own hands after only a few months in those islands, said, "I should have gone mad and died beside that lonely grave if it had not been for Christ and the presence he vouchsafed to me there." Yet it is also true that the real proving-ground of human character is not crisis but routine.

Erosion takes longer than explosion, but in the long run the effect can be as devastating. Many a man, many a married couple can rise to a crisis by sheer strength of character; but it takes something stronger than character to stay with life's routine situations—exhausting work, home duties, unhappy relationships, the care of sick people, the business of making ends meet. It takes stamina, resilience and an infinite capacity for inward renewal; it takes all the resources of religion.

That is exactly what those resources are for. The fortieth chapter of Isaiah seems to close with an anti-climax: "They that wait upon the Lord shall renew their strength; they shall mount up with wings as eagles; they shall run, and not be weary; and they shall walk, and not faint." Soaring, running, walking! But shouldn't the order be reversed? Simply to plod along from day to day without fainting hardly seems an exciting, challenging ultimate result of faith. Not exciting, perhaps, but true to life. To be sure, life has its soaring flights and breathless sprints, but how often do we have to fly or run? Most of the time we walk, following the daily schedule called "routine". We get up at the same hour in the same reluctant way, eat the same breakfast in the same sullen silence, take the same route to the same building to greet the same people and cope with the same duties that we faced yesterday. Anti-climax or not, it was sheer realism that impelled the prophet to offer the supreme resource of religious faith for that which most of us do most of the time: "They shall walk and not faint."

Turning from the illusions of our culture to the reality of the Bible, we notice that *the purpose of religion is not only to redeem us from our moral failures but to keep us from failing in the first place.*

The illusion is that, in order to need or want religion, you have to be what the Prayer Book calls a "miserable sinner" You have to be lost in the wilderness of the world's disgust or trapped in the dark pit of self-loathing. You have to be morally shipwrecked, clinging to a spar and certain to drown unless some supernatural arm throws out a life-belt and pulls you to safety. As long as you lead a decent life and keep out of prison, as long as other people respect you and you respect yourself, then you no more need religion than a healthy man needs an ambulance.

Again we acknowledge gratefully that the Christian religion does have marvellous redemptive power and that the arm of the Good Shepherd reaches down to retrieve his lost sheep from the rocky precipice of hell. Yet it were sheer unrealism to think of hell only in terms of a precipice. Someone has said that the most travelled roads to hell are the undramatic, gentle slopes. Through the years, and without noticing, our little personal prejudices develop into hardened habits of hatred. Daily unimportant pamperings of our senses grow unperceived into insatiable appetites for wrong. The slender string of self-seeking binds our spirits with a selfishness that holds us in its grip. It is from these little evils that quietly assault our souls, not from some slimy pit of self-destruction, that we need our religion to save us.

The Parable of the Prodigal Son brings tears to the eyes. We cannot read our Lord's tender story of the foolish lad who left his father's home and heart, squandered his money in a far country, crawled the gutter of degradation, came to himself and returned home to be welcomed and forgiven—without getting all choked up with emotion. We weep because we know instinctively that the Prodigal is every man and that God is the forgiving Father who always welcomes us home from the far country of moral folly. Yet there is something that might have been more glorious than the Prodigal's reclamation from the far country, and that is that he should never have gone there in the first place. We should be denied the excitement and the emotion of it, because nothing moves us like a story of rescue; but a far finer fruit of religion than the sight of men and women dragged out of moral hell is the sight of men and women who never get into moral hell because, sustained by a lively faith in God and a close comradeship with Christ, they live honourable and useful lives.

Harry Emerson Fosdick wrote a memorable sermon entitled "Preventive Religion".[1] Taking as his text the fine, familiar benediction from the Epistle of Jude, "Now unto him that is able to keep you from falling", he develops the theme that religion is not simply a rescue party waiting at the foot of a precipice to pick up those who have fallen over; it is a fence at the top to prevent their falling over in the first place. He finds a parallel in the shift of emphasis from curative to preventive medicine, recalling the revolution in science begun by Louis Pasteur when it was discovered that not only could men be cured of a disease; they could be immunized, so that the disease had no more dominion over them. Having been innoculated, they could walk in its presence unafraid and uncontaminated. That, declares Dr. Fosdick, is the purpose of religion—not only to cure us when we are morally ill but to keep us healthy, to give us through faith in God and friendship with Christ a kind of spiritual immunity to the diseases that decimate society and imperil our souls.

Reading the Bible carefully, we notice further that *the*

[1] *Riverside Sermons*, Harper & Brothers, New York, 1958, p. 83 ff.

purpose of religion is not just to overcome our weaknesses but to perfect our strength.

The Church itself must accept some of the blame for its own distorted image because the Church, in attempting to popularize the Gospel, has too often presented it as nothing but a pink pill for personality problems. You know the approach: "You worry? Try the tranquillizer of trust. You feel guilty? Take a dose of God's forgiveness. You feel frustrated? Get an injection of faith. You lack self-confidence? Let religion build you up." This morbid preoccupation with personality problems, to the exclusion of positive Christian duty in the Church and the world, may in the long run have done the cause of Christ more harm than good. Surely it encourages the illusion that Christianity is primarily a religion for weaklings, that one has to be a bit neurotic before it becomes relevant to his condition, and that the Gospel has nothing to say to people who are strong, successful, well-adjusted and happy.

Religion does have tremendous therapeutic power. Many, whose own resources proved insufficient, have returned to their religious faith with a new earnestness and found it a source of strength which restored their self-confidence and brought them victoriously through times of stress. To her minister's vestry comes a woman with twitching face and trembling hands who bursts into tears as she crushes out her half-smoked cigarette. She has lost her grip on life. She is an emotional wreck. Patiently the minister listens to her. Gently he probes the reason for her anxiety. Quietly he mediates the healing ministry of Christ, until one day tears of another kind flow down her cheeks, tears of gladness and gratitude that wash the feet of an invisible Saviour.

Yet, to suppose that the Christian religion caters only to

emotional weakness were to ignore the more masculine teachings of Jesus which, while they contain much to console the sorrowful and restore the defeated, contain even more that speaks to the strong, successful, self-reliant members of society. Jesus directed his ministry not only to publicans and prostitutes; he said some direct things to lawyers and priests and big men of business and people in their ordinary occupations. And what of his own disciples? What were they to do? They were to suffer for righteousness' sake; they were to turn the other cheek and go the second mile; they were to love their enemies and pray for those who persecuted them; they were to go out as sheep in the midst of wolves; they were to be hated of all men for his name's sake. Does that sound like a religion for weaklings? Is it not rather a Gospel for the strong, intended to perfect their strength?

What else can we expect from the virile Man of Nazareth? Was he himself not the strongest of men? In his mastery over the demoniac, his silencing of a storm, his cleansing of the temple, his dignity before Caiaphas, his sanity in suffering and his courageous endurance of a tortured death—does he not give the impression of phenomenal strength? "Behold the man!" declared Pontius Pilate who spoke in larger terms than he realized, for it was the manhood of the Master that magnetized men, the glory of his full-orbed personality, the fact that when he submitted to the will of God he obeyed not out of weakness but out of strength. It is a caricature of the Church that offers itself only as a spiritual nursing-home for emotional invalids. The Church, as long as it remains loyal to the teaching and character of Jesus, will always be an army for strong soldiers, intended to perfect their strength in the service of God.

. . . . .

We notice from the Bible that *the purpose of religion is not only to comfort us in our afflictions but to afflict us in our comfort.*

Another illusion entertained by some of the spokesmen of our culture is the illusion of infallibility. (It could profitably be the subject of an additional chapter.) Particularly prone to it are those pundits of the Press and the radio who consider themselves the final authority on a variety of subjects and indulgently instruct us peasants on "the way things really are". In Canada a few years ago, one of them published an indictment of the Church called *The Comfortable Pew*[1] which mainly created the impression that the author had not been in many church pews, else he would have known that even in a material sense pews are notoriously uncomfortable, especially towards the close of a long sermon. Even a cushioned pew can make its occupant squirm if public worship brings him into the presence of God and if the man in the pulpit speaks directly to him from the Word of God. That Word may be a healing balm to his sin-sick soul; it may also be a sharp sword that stabs his sleeping conscience and shows him the sinner that he really is.

Possibly the deluded journalist was misled by the "Peace of Mind" cult which was popular in the 1950's, though how it ever crept into the thinking of Christians remains a mystery. You find peace of mind in some religious paper-backs; you do not find it in the Bible, least of all in the teachings of Jesus. His Gospel is not a sedative but a stimulant. Rather than eliminating tension, it creates tension. Instead of removing the agony from life, it puts agony into life. Far from pouring oil on troubled waters, it stirs up a storm in the souls of men.

[1] Pierre Berton, *The Comfortable Pew*, McClelland and Stewart, Limited, Toronto, 1965.

To be sure, there is much in the Christian religion to comfort our afflictions, but there is even more to afflict our comfort; and if we encounter the radical Christ of God we shall find him to be no popular preacher counselling us to relax but a lonely, unpopular man treading the dark road of Calvary and commanding us to follow him.

Because the Church seems to have fallen on lean years, some of its leaders in Britain proposed that the Church enlist the services of a professional public relations agency in order to regain public support. A cartoon in *Punch* satirized the proposal. It showed the experts smoking furiously in a "think-session", and one of them saying, "What we need is an image." What he doesn't know is that the Church *has* an image. It has had that image for nineteen centuries, and the image has never changed. It is the image of a man dying on a Cross and saying to the whole world, "Whoever would come after me, let him deny himself and take up his cross and follow me." Not a comfortable image, but it has worked, and there is no Christianity without it.

Anyone who turns to the Christian religion under the illusion that it dispenses only comfort is bound to be uncomfortably disillusioned. Ernest Gordon in his distinguished book, *Through the Valley of the Kwai*,[1] describing his internment in a Japanese prison camp, tells how the diseased, depressed, hopeless prisoners of war turned to religion, looking for help outside themselves. They attended open-air services, sang hymns lustily, read their Bibles and prayed fervently. Captain Gordon says that they did this, in the first instance, as a measure of desperation, an attempt to find comfort and, if possible, persuade God to rescue them from the miseries of their prison existence. They turned to God and

[1] Harper & Row, Publishers, New York and Evanston, 1962.

said, in effect, "Look, old boy, I'm in trouble. I'll speak well of you if you'll get me out of this." But God didn't get them out, not then, and soon they were disillusioned. They had turned to religion as a crutch, but the crutch had not supported them, so they threw it away.

Some time later there came a true awakening of faith among these hopeless prisoners of war. It came not by human initiative but by a movement of God's Spirit and it found expression not in piety but in Christian love and service. The men now helped one another to live, they worked for the common good, and some even laid down their lives for others. The whole life of the camp was transformed. Why? Because even these disease-ridden skeletons were red-blooded men who responded more to a religion of sacrifice than to a religion of comfort. In their jungle hell, where there are no illusions, they faced up to the fact that religion can never be an escape-hatch and that faith finds fruition not in comfort but in power.

CHAPTER 13

THE ILLUSION OF INNOCENCE

A dramatic scene in Rolf Hochhuth's play, *The Representative* brings into focus another of the great illusions of our culture. Father Riccardo Fontana, a young Jesuit priest stationed in Germany during World War Two, agonizes over the suffering of the Jews. Wearing a Star of David on his cassock, he seeks an audience with Pope Pius XII in Rome and pleads with the Holy Father to use his great influence to stop the atrocities. After listening patiently, His Holiness explains that there is nothing he can do and he admonishes the young priest to return to his duties and cease being emotionally involved with the persecuted people. When Riccardo protests, the Pope dismisses him. Meanwhile a monk, bearing a basin of water and a towel, has glided into the papal chamber. Silently the Pope washes his trembling hands in the basin.

We are told that it was a characteristic gesture of Pius XII who had an excessive mania for hygiene and who had his hands disinfected after every audience. At once, however, we see a parallel with an incident in the New Testament. After Pontius Pilate, the Roman Governor of Judea, had surrendered to the pressure of the priests and sentenced Jesus to be crucified, even though he knew that the prisoner was not guilty of a capital crime, he called for a basin of water. There on the balcony of his imperial palace in full view of the priests and the crucifixion mob he washed his hands in the basin and cried out, "I am innocent of this man's blood; see to it yourselves." (Matthew 27:24.) The mob shouted its approval.

But posterity has not shouted its approval. To Pilate's preposterous plea, "I am innocent", all history and all men of good conscience have retorted, "Oh yeah! Innocent, when you gave the order for his execution? Innocent, when you could have set him free? You told him so yourself, 'Do you not know that I have power to release you, and power to crucify you?' (John 19:10.) Come off it, Pilate. You're not innocent. You're as guilty as hell!" And maybe Pilate, now within the shades of eternity, hangs his head in shamed agreement. Perhaps Pilate, wherever he is in God's universe, still carries on his conscience the burden of his cowardly action. In Switzerland there is a mountain named Mount Pilatus. They say that over the waters of Lake Lucerne at the foot of this mountain you can see Pilate's ghost on moonlight nights, for ever moaning, for ever washing his hands. Nothing can cleanse the guilt of his tormented soul.

Pilate is a "representative" in that he personifies one of the big illusions of our culture. It is the illusion of innocence, the mistaken idea that individuals or groups of people can somehow dissociate themselves and wash their hands from the corporate guilt of collective crime. It is a childish illusion that takes hold of us when we are very young. Because we didn't actually throw the ball that smashed a neighbour's window we rush away from the ball game, crying out, "I didn't do it! It wasn't my fault! I am innocent!" Because we didn't actually participate in the classroom riot during the teacher's absence we quickly protest, "I didn't start it, teacher. I am innocent!" Some people never outgrow the illusion. They know that the world in which they live is a mess but they accept no responsibility for the world's evil and suffering. Let others bear the blame. As for the self-righteous ones, they wash their hands and cry out in many tongues and accents, "We are innocent!"

Some of the spokesmen in our culture encourage the illusion of innocence. On a college campus in the United States the chaplains of the several faiths drafted a statement for circulation among the faculty which invited them to sign their names to a manifesto on civil rights, especially for disadvantaged racial and ethnic groups in American society. The statement spoke to Americans of their "national guilt" in the treatment of these groups, a guilt which academic institutions were alleged to share. The faculty, however, did not like this reference to collective guilt. Several members of the History Department, remembering the disruptive effect of the idea of "war guilt" in European politics following World War One, declined to endorse the statement. A distinguished author of studies in the work of Sigmund Freud gave his judgment that the whole idea of guilt was too disturbing emotionally. He insisted that a cool head rather than a penitent heart would be more useful in moving America towards a resolution of her racial problems. Like many spokesmen of our culture they preferred to cling to the illusion of innocence.[1]

Once in a long while someone writes a book which is really verbal dynamite that blasts the illusion of innocence into a thousand fragments. Such a book is *We, The Crucifiers*,[2] written by the English author, G. W. Target. His theme is an old one—the identification of ourselves with the executioners of Christ—but never has that theme been more realistically and

[1] Told by John M. Krumm in *The Art of Being a Sinner*, The Seabury Press, New York, 1967, pp. 20–21.
[2] Hodder and Stoughton, London, 1964.

devastatingly presented. Target, in his strange rhetorical style, presents the Passion narrative in a series of up-to-date episodes, showing us that we are the actors in the drama. We are the sleeping Church in the Garden of Gethsemane, the religious establishment that protects religion at the expense of Christianity, the ranting mob that prefers a common criminal to the best of men. We are the crucifiers of Christ.

We *are* the crucifiers. That is the point of Target's book. It's not that we *were* "there when they crucified my Lord". We *are* there, because Calvary is not only past history; it is also present reality. The Crucifixion of Christ not only happened; it happens. The corporate crime of deicide, from which a latter-day Pope unnecessarily absolved the Jews, is the very crime that Christians have committed against Jews, the crime that lies at the root of all collective tragedy in the world today. We all share the guilt of that corporate crime. Indeed, who among us would presume to plead innocence and dare to claim that his hands are clean?

Whose hands are not soiled with the *cowardice* of Pontius Pilate? Who would not have acted as he did under the circumstances? He was simply protecting his own interests, simply saving his own skin, and few people would blame him for that. Pilate had no quarrel with Jesus. Everything indicates that he respected the prisoner and tried to get him acquitted because he saw the prisoner's innocence as clearly as he saw through the trumped-up charges against him. But Pilate saw also that Caiaphas, the High Priest, was determined to have the death sentence, and Caiaphas was Caesar's stool-pigeon, and Pilate knew that if he didn't co-operate in this intrigue, Caesar would hear about it, and he might lose his job, possibly his head. Why support a lost cause anyway? Society had already condemned Jesus. One way or another he would go down, and it would be sheer suicide to go down with him.

Self -preservation! Is that not the motive that lies hidden in the heart of the great crime of racism? Is it not the motive behind immigration quotas and policies of racial segregation? Is it not the material of which barriers are built that imprison people in ghettos where they are denied their basic rights as human beings? Self-preservation! Is it not the motive that makes cowards of us all? We don't hate the minority groups in our society, but society keeps them in their place, and it seems suicidal for us to beat our heads against the stone wall of human prejudice. Like Pilate we see no gain for ourselves in supporting an unpopular cause. Perhaps we are the "nodders" of whom a courageous journalist wrote when he said that Martin Luther King was executed by a firing squad that numbered in the millions. The man with the gun did what he was told, but behind him were the bigots who put the gun in his hand and told him that he was doing the right thing. And behind the bigots "were the subtle ones, those who never say anything bad but just nod when the bigot throws out his strong opinions. He is actually worse, the nodder is, because sometimes he believes differently but he says nothing. He doesn't want to cause trouble . . ."

Whose hands are not soiled with the *violence* of the Roman soldiers who scourged the Strong Son of God and hammered huge spikes through his quivering flesh? They also might protest their personal innocence and argue that, like Pilate, they had no quarrel with Jesus; they were simply carrying out orders. Nazi officers at Nuremburg made the same plea of personal innocence; they also protested that they were simply carrying out orders when they herded Jews into gas chambers. The Chicago police sang the same tune when the public conscience accused them of excessive brutality against the peaceful demonstrators at the Democratic Convention in 1968. But the Chicago police and the Nazis and the Roman soldiers showed the world that the line between carrying out orders and violence for the sake of violence is very thin. They showed us that an ugly streak of violence runs through human nature, sometimes erupting in brutality, insurrection and war; and it's an illusion to suppose that we are innocent of it.

Because the Christian Pavilion at Expo 67 in Montreal shattered the illusion of innocence, many people reacted negatively to the Pavilion. Some disliked it intensely and expressed their dislike in vehement terms. The first of the three "zones" depicted our common life with all its interrelationships in the good world which God has created, and we found it pleasingly neutral. Descending by a carpeted ramp to the second zone, we found the prospect changing, and with it our mood underwent a change. Stark and brutal photographs presented a picture of the mess that man makes of his world and of his relationships when he cannot control his violent passions. In a small, dark, confining room we saw a short black-and-white film which showed dictators mouthing their blasphemies, one war after another desecrating human persons, victims trying to stop weeping, peacemakers failing to end the horrors. We couldn't get out of there fast enough, not because the scenes of violence sickened us but because we could not dissociate ourselves from this spectacle of infamy. We felt involved in it, responsible for it, and a dead weight of guilt rested heavily on our hearts.

Whose hands are not soiled with the *hypocrisy* of the priests? Never from human lips has there issued such a masterpiece of hypocrisy as that uttered by Caiaphas when he justified the monstrous crime about to be committed by saying unctuously

". . . it is expedient . . . that one man should die for the people, and that the whole nation should not perish". (John 11:50.) In his powerful play, *The Visit*, Friedrich Duerrenmatt clothes the hypocrisy of the priests in modern dress. He tells the story of a small town in Europe which has gone economically bankrupt. Only one person can save the population from extinction and that person is a fabulously rich woman who left the town many years before and plans to return for a visit. She arrives with her weird entourage, she offers to put the town on its feet again and she stipulates her price. It must be the life of the leading citizen who made her pregnant and deserted her when she was a girl. The town fathers are shocked by her outrageous demand. Murder a man? Unthinkable! Gradually, however, their thinking changes, and one after another the various elements in society—the law, the school, business, the town council, the Church, even the man's family—decide that one person's life is not an unreasonable price to pay for the common good. In the end they murder him, secure now in their prosperity and their hypocrisy.

Such dramas take place on the stage of real life. Macaulay once said that there is no spectacle more ridiculous than the British people in one of their periodical fits of morality. He should have seen the British people a few years ago when their slumbering Puritanism was stabbed broad awake by one of the worst political scandals in living memory. It centred on the conduct of one man, a Minister of the Crown who betrayed the confidence of his constituents, his colleagues and his country. Bitingly Lord Hailsham referred to the scandal as "a squalid affair between a woman of easy virtue and a proved liar". Somehow this "squalid affair" of lust and deceit brought to the surface all the accumulated filth that lies on the river-bed of society, and high-minded people recoiled with disgust. Yet there were those who detected an undercurrent of hypocrisy in this public outcry. Mr. Selwyn Lloyd punctured the illusion of innocence when he said, "None of us are blameless in this matter: the Government, Parliament, the Church, the Press, and the great majority of ordinary folk. We are all in some degree responsible, and we cannot quieten our consciences by seeking to make scapegoats of particular individuals."

Whose hands are not soiled with the *callousness* of the crowds on Calvary? They, among all the actors in the Passion drama, might justifiably plead their innocence. They were not actors, were they? They were spectators in the audience, helpless spectators. They had no control over the action taking place on the stage. They didn't write the play, didn't direct it, didn't even participate in it. There was nothing they could do but stand by and watch.

Isn't that exactly the illusion of innocence? It is the repudiation of our social solidarity. It is the mistaken idea that in a world which, according to the experts, contains enough latent resources to support twice its present population, we can stand by and watch 480 million people living on the brink of starvation and 12,000 dying daily of hunger. To be sure, we are not directly responsible for the gigantic crime of world poverty but can we wash our hands of it? On a single day (July 9th, 1968) the Toronto *Globe and Mail* published three items. The first told the familiar, grim story of starvation in Biafra, the story of people too weakened by hunger to flee from their pursuers, babies sucking on the wizened dry breasts of their mothers, vultures circling overhead and waiting to descend on a human meal. On the same page, right next to the Biafra story, was an appetizing restaurant advertisement inviting Toronto business men to relax in the oak-panelled dining-room and enjoy an elegant two-hour lunch with exotic menu and fine wines. On another page was the report of a speech by U Thant, Secretary-General of the U.N.O., who predicted that failure to assist poorer nations to bridge the gap separating them from the rich countries is "an invitation to violence". Can we, living in a comparatively affluent society, claim that our hands are clean?

We can thank God that not all the voices in our culture encourage the illusion of innocence. There are poets, artists, journalists and novelists who consciously or unconsciously acknowledge that Christ is still crucified and that the crimes which crucify him every day have their roots in the human heart. So declares Kenneth Fearing:

"'Guilt', said John, 'is always and everywhere nothing less than guilt.
I have always, at all times, been a willing accomplice of the crass and the crude.
I have overheard, daily, the smallest details of conspiracies against the human race, vast in their ultimate scope, and conspired, daily, to launch my own.
You have heard of innocent men who died in the chair.
It was my avarice that threw the switch.
I helped, and I do not deny it, to nail that guy to the cross, and shall continue to help.
Look into my eyes, you can see the guilt.
Look at my face, my hair, my very clothing, you will see guilt written plainly everywhere.
Guilt of the flesh. Of the soul. Of eating, when others do not.
Of breathing and laughing and sleeping.

> I am guilty of what? Of guilt. Guilty of guilt, that is all, and enough'."[1]

"How utterly degrading!" cries the humanist. "How vulgar and crude! What possible good can accrue to the human race from this morbid and unhealthy obsession with guilt?" We shall not deny that an obsession with guilt may do psychological harm to the individual unless he has the spiritual resources for dealing with it. We shall insist, however, that in the relationships of society the sense of guilt is not unhealthy and that greater harm is done by its absence in the illusion of innocence. It was not a preacher addressing a congregation but a member of the House of Lords who said in a lecture to the British Psycho-Analytical Society: "If with the wave of a psycho-analytical wand you could abolish tomorrow the sense of guilt in the human mind, it would cause an instantaneous collapse of law and order." To cling to the illusion of innocence is human; to cease feeling guilty is to cease being a responsible member of human society.

People who try to keep up the illusion of innocence cut themselves off not only from society but also from God. That may not matter too much to the humanist as long as he has other means of dealing with his personal and corporate failure. It matters supremely to the Christian because, cut off from God, he is cut off from the only means of redeeming his personal and corporate failures. To bring God into the picture makes our situation worse, because then the sense of guilt becomes something more serious—a sense of sin against God. Yet, to bring God into the picture also makes our situation better, because now a new possibility comes into view—

[1] From "Confession Overheard in a Subway" in *Afternoon of a Pawnbroker and Other Poems*, copyright, 1943, by Kenneth Fearing. Reprinted by permission of Harcourt, Brace & World, Inc.

the possibility of God's grace. That grace may appear to us as judgment, but even as judgment it is still grace, and we can still pray, "Forgive us our sins."

Those who acknowledge no involvement in the crimes that crucify Christ have no knowledge of what the Cross of Christ is all about. They don't feel judged by the Cross; so, of course, they feel no sense of guilt over it. They don't know that the Cross is God's way of exposing and dealing with our guilt; it is God's ultimate act in history which shows how seriously he takes our guilt; it is the price that God pays to lift from our souls the burden of guilt. The illusion of innocence in our culture is really tied to the collapse of the Christian Faith. It may be that we need to get things the other way round and look first at God, then at ourselves; first at his grace, then at our guilt; first at the Cross, then at our illusion of innocence and recognize it as an illusion.

CHAPTER 14

THE ILLUSION OF IMMORTALITY

"The illusion of immortality" is a phrase that keeps recurring in the novels of Morris West. In *Daughter of Silence*, the author describes an ageing man sitting for his portrait as "an exercise in futility, an illusion of immortality to which he submitted himself with irony". In *The Shoes of the Fisherman*, he notes as one of the forms of the impulse to survival "the delight in power which gives a man the illusion of immortality". The phrase occurs even more pointedly in *The Devil's Advocate* where he writes of the priest who learned from his doctor that he had only a few months to live:

> "He was a resonable man and reason told him that a man's death sentence is written on his palm the day he is born; he was a cold man, little troubled by passion, irked not at all by discipline, yet his first impulse had been a wild clinging to the illusion of immortality."[1]

The illusion, simply stated, is the refusal to face up to the fact of death. In our sober moments, and especially as our aches and pains become more frequent, we are prepared to admit that each day we die a little and that in this uncertain

[1] Dell Publishing Co., Inc., New York, 1959, p. 5.

world death is the only thing of which we can be 100 per cent certain. We know that sooner or later, by violent or peaceful means, singly or in wholesale lots, we have a rendezvous with death. We believe it at the top of our minds but we don't really accept it at the bottom of our hearts. In spite of the most convincing evidence that life on this earth comes to an end, we try to convince ourselves that life goes on for ever. We cling to the illusion of immortality.

The illusion takes various forms. Sometimes it takes the form of a conspiracy of silence, the inability to discuss the subject of death naturally or the unwillingness to talk about it at all. In the home parents try to prepare their children for all of life's experiences, yet they think that they are doing the youngsters a kindness by saying nothing about the inevitable experience of death. A child asks, "Where is Grandpa?" and his mother replies, "Grandpa's gone away, dear". Afterwards she tells a neighbour, "We didn't take the children to the funeral. We want them to remember their grandfather as he was." Some people will not discuss death even when their own death or the death of a loved one is imminent, and that is a sad state of affairs because it means that, though we comfort one another in fond farewells before travelling abroad on the earth, we haven't the courage to comfort one another and say good-bye before travelling abroad to eternity.

The illusion of immortality shows itself in our pathetic efforts to disguise the ageing process. Manufacturers of cosmetics have amassed fortunes by selling products to people who want to camouflage the fact that they are growing old. It is by no means a modern trick. Dickens in his *Dombey and Son* has a character, Mrs. Skewton, who died, much to the surprise of her friends; though they needn't have been surprised, because she was really a very old woman who disguised her age with consummate cleverness. Dickens describes her personal maid removing the various disguises at the end of the day and putting what was left of her mistress to bed:

> "The painted object shrivelled underneath her hand; the form collapsed, the hair dropped off, the arched dark eyebrows changed to scanty tufts of grey; the pale lips shrunk, the skin became cadaverous and loose; an old, worn, yellow nodding woman, with red eyes, alone remained in Cleopatra's place, huddled up, like a slovenly bundle, in a greasy flannel gown."

The illusion shows itself in our frantic efforts to prolong life by a few years. Eagerly we welcome every advance in medical science, every new miracle drug which promises to arrest a disease or slow down the ageing process or in some way grant us a series of short reprieves. We know that these discoveries which lengthen life do not change our essential situation. We die eventually anyway—all that remains to be settled is the date—but there are some who would try to change even that inexorable fact. The Russians, of all people, with a curious disregard of the problems of the population explosion, have set up a scientific Faculty of Immortality whose director says, "We are searching for the right chemicals to introduce into the human body to interrupt the whole process of ageing and death." In the United States there is a Life Extension Society with headquarters in Washington that provides its members with a "freezer card" which indicates their desire at death to have their bodies put into cold storage and kept frozen, at a cost of several thousand dollars, until medical science can cure them of disease or old age and bring them back to life. Visitors will be allowed to view their relatives in these time-capsule cemeteries by means of closed-circuit television.

The illusion of immortality takes a more implicit and serious form. It is seen in the man who lives dangerously, drives himself like a machine, builds up no estate and takes out no life insurance, even though he knows that his wife and family will be destitute in the event of his death. It is seen in the business executive who keeps the affairs of his firm under tight personal control, knowing all the time that complete chaos will result if he is suddenly taken out of the picture. It is seen in the statesman who refuses to delegate authority or appoint a successor, although he needs no imagination to foresee the struggle for power that will take place when he finally passes from the scene. Such people, whatever they believe with their minds, order their lives as if they were like Tennyson's little brook: "For men may come and men may go, but I go on for ever." All of them and many others like them cling to the illusion of immortality.

A single verse in the New Testament shatters the illusion of immortality: "Go to now, ye that say, Today or tomorrow we will go into such a city, and continue there a year, and buy and sell, and get gain: Whereas ye know not what shall be on the morrow. For what is your life? It is even a vapour, that appeareth for a little time, and then vanisheth away." (James 4:13, 14.)

We accept that obvious truth as far as other people are concerned. We have to. Every day we pick up the newspaper and read in the obituary column the names of people whom we knew very well, strong, healthy people who told us only a week ago of their plans to buy and sell and get gain; but yesterday death rudely interrupted those plans, and today they have vanished like a vapour. Suppose we accept the truth for ourselves? Suppose, after reading the obituary column, we say honestly, "One of these days *my* name is going to be in the newspaper"? Suppose we come to terms with the fact that these mortal bodies in which we live are as perishable as houses that can be demolished by disaster or that simply grow old and crumble and finally fall to the ground? Suppose deep down in our hearts we admit to ourselves that life comes to an end just as a journey comes to an end, what difference will it make to our attitudes and our behaviour?

At the very least, we shall develop a healthier respect for time, knowing that our supply of that precious commodity is not unlimited and that some day the supply will run out. Most people discover that truth gradually, and the discovery is not always a happy one. The youth, who thinks that he has for ever to complete his education and sponge off his parents and sow his wild oats, wakes up one morning to find that he is a man and that the world expects him to act like a man and shoulder a man's responsibilities. Parents, who think that they have for ever to bring up their children, suddenly discover that the children have grown into adults with minds and wills of their own and that the days of parental discipline are over. A man with great ambitions for his career comes to middle-age only to find that the world now looks to the younger generation; or he comes to retirement and discovers to his dismay that he hasn't the strength and energy for all the things that he had planned to do in retirement. Time runs out. That's what Jesus meant by his parable of the prosperous farmer to whom God said, "Fool! This night your soul is required of you; and the things you have prepared, whose will they be?" (Luke 12:20.) Not that God planned to kill him off;

it was just that his time had run out; and once we come to terms with that obvious fact we shall treat time with a healthier respect and try to make the most of it.

Thornton Wilder teaches that lesson in his play, *Our Town*, where Emily Gibbs, who died giving birth to her baby, comes back to earth and watches herself re-living the morning of her twelfth birthday. It is an excited occasion at the breakfast table with presents and greeting cards and kisses from her parents and brothers and sisters. But all the people in the house, her childhood self included, are rushing about, scarcely paying attention to one another. Suddenly from the unseen she begs them to stop and cries out, "Just for a moment we're happy. Let's look at one another." But the living are too busy, so Emily sadly bids the earth a last farewell, "Oh, earth, you're too wonderful for anyone to realize you." Turning to the stage manager, she asks through her tears, "Do any human beings ever realize life while they live it—every, every minute?" That philosopher answers, "No, the Saints and Poets, maybe—they do some."

Once we get rid of the illusion that we are immortal we shall then face up to the reality of death. Medical science helps us to do so in these days when doctors are transplanting human organs from one body to another, and the question has to be asked, "When can a patient be pronounced dead—when his brain stops functioning or when his heart stops beating?" However morbid the issue, it punctures the illusion of immortality by bringing death out into the open and compelling us to reckon with it as an inescapable experience that happens to all of us, an experience that we have to go though like getting an education or having a tooth extracted.

Some churches sponsor programmes for "senior citizens" which include the discussion of hobbies, health, finances, housing and other topics that directly concern older adults in their years of retirement. In 1965 a group at the Riverside Church in New York began pioneering in a field which most churches seem reluctant to touch—a frank and honest discussion of death and related topics. They called it the "Plan Now—Retire Later" programme. Consisting of a series of lectures by distinguished doctors, psychiatrists, theologians and pastors, it made an instant appeal not only to elderly folk but also to single young adults, middle-aged married couples, the rich and the poor. In fact, the whole programme was so enthusiastically received that inquiries came from as far as the Philippines, and a New York newspaper made it the subject of a lead editorial. In an atmosphere not of gloomy emotion but of calm consideration 250 persons talked about preparation for death and bereavement as naturally and rationally as others would talk about preparing for marriage and parenthood. They did not cling to the illusion of immortality.

It would make an immense difference to our outlook on life if we could face up to death with that kind of courageous realism. It would bring enormous comfort to those whom we leave behind, saving them from the guilt of things undone and the regret of things unsaid. It would strengthen our spirits as we grow old or suffer from an illness that may or may not be curable. Here in the pages of a British magazine is the confession of an old man who, as he sensed that his time was running out, looked into the face of death calmly and realistically:

"I have been told by experts that I have cancer of the lung and that at my age (81) it is not possible to operate. I feel it right, therefore, to try to tell, in this brief manifesto, my

> own final faith in the face of this final crisis of my life . . . This final faith is, for me, both a rational and a revealed reconception that . . . death is not defeat, but creative deed, its dark night not extinction but the womb of new life and light. It is therefore potentially the most momentous deed a man can do . . . By virtue of this faith thus inherited from my Christian tradition but also hammered out on the anvil of a long life and many crises, I go . . . to my encounter with this ordeal of death with gladness . . ."[1]

But what if that also is an illusion, the biggest illusion of all? Since ancient times and in all cultures men have clung stubbornly to a larger belief in immortality—the invincible surmise that, though the body grows old and decays, the soul, the personality, the individual self survives. "John Brown's body lies a-mould'ring in the grave. His soul goes marching on." Philosophers have piled up their arguments for the immortality of the soul. Christians have clung to it as their supreme source of comfort in the dark valley of bereavement. Even men who were not religious in their lifetimes have refused to let it go. Mark Twain, though he grew terribly bitter and cynical in his later years, confessed to a friend, "I don't understand it; I've successfully exploded every possible argument for an after-life, and in spite of that I fully expect there to be one." Is that also an illusion that can be punctured with the sword of Holy Scripture?

We had better be candid at this point. The Bible does not set out to shatter the hope of immortality, as we understand it, but neither does the Bible specifically support that hope as we understand it. The Bible says nothing about the popular

[1] "An Old Man's Manifesto", Published in *The New Christian*, 30 May, 1968, p. 5.

belief in the immortality of the soul because the Bible does not divide man into body and soul; the distinction is a pagan one. The Bible sees man in his totality. If a man lives, the whole man lives, and if a man dies, the whole man dies. Therefore, if we look to the Bible as our final court of appeal in the ultimate questions about life and death, we shall be forced to admit that even in a larger sense immortality is an illusion.

That seems to make the Bible an inconsistent book, not only inconsistent but cruel. When we turn to the Bible in our times of grief, does it not assure us, often in appealingly pictorial language, that those whom we have loved and lost are not annihilated; they are still real, they still belong to us, still love us, still reach out to help us, they even wait for us on "another shore"? Most assuredly the Bible says all of that and says so without corroborating our popular belief in the immortality of the soul. The Bible takes away the illusion that within us there is something imperishable, something inherently immortal, something which survives death as naturally as a dragon-fly survives the cracked-open shell of a beetle. Then, in place of the illusion, the Bible gives us a more credible hope, a hope based not on human surmise but on a historical event. That event is the resurrection of Jesus Christ from the dead.

We must be very clear what the Bible says about the resurrection of Jesus. First, it says that Jesus was dead and that everything about him was dead. Even he did not possess a built-in mortality, so that, while his body lay a-mould'ring in Joseph's sepulchre, his soul went marching on. Then it says that Jesus returned from the dead. He lived again and appeared to his disciples, so that they recognized him and trusted his promise, "Because I live, you will live also." (John 14:19.) There can be only one explanation. The popular belief in immortality places its trust in man; it asserts that we shall live beyond the grave because we are incapable of dying. The Christian belief in resurrection places its trust in God; it asserts that we shall live beyond the grave because God in his mighty love and loving might raises us from death to life. That is what the Bible says about Jesus. It says that, though he was dead, God raised him from the dead. His resurrection was a mighty act of God.

Near a park in Melbourne, Australia, there is a small statue of a donkey bearing a wounded soldier on its back. Standing beside it is another soldier, in a uniform of the First World War, with his arm around the shoulder of his wounded comrade. That man's name was John Simpson Kirkpatrick, a plain private in the Australian army, an ordinary man who did extraordinary things in a critical situation. At the ill-conceived landing on Gallipoli the allied forces suffered heavy casualties. Wounded men were left to die in the field, because there was no means of transporting them to the casualty clearing station on the beach. Then this stretcher-bearer, Kirkpatrick, found a donkey and got the idea that it would make a good ambulance. For twenty-four days and nights he travelled up and down a shrapnel-swept gulley transporting wounded men on the back of his donkey. He saved hundreds of lives. It was a heroic and dangerous thing to do. The Indians called him "Bahadur", which means "bravest of the brave". His comrades affectionately nick-named him "Murphy". Officers and men loved this familiar Good Samaritan of Shrapnel Gulley, who spoke so tenderly to the wounded and the dying, but they knew what the end would be—an enemy machine-gun bullet in his heart. When the officer commanding the Indian Field Ambulance received word that Kirkpatrick had been killed he did something that astonished all who knew him. He covered his face with his hands and prayed aloud, "O God, if ever a man deserves Heaven, he does. Give it to him!" "Where's Murphy?" asked a British private who had not heard the tragic news. A sergeant replied, "Murphy's at Heaven's gate, helping the wounded soldiers through."

That is the Christian answer to the illusion of immortality: not an argument which anyone with normal intelligence can punch full of holes; not an argument but a hope that God who raised Jesus from the dead will raise us with Jesus if we are identified with him; not an argument but a decision to believe in Jesus and trust him and follow him and accept him as Saviour and Lord.

[1] The full story of John Simpson Kirkpatrick is told by Sir Irving Benson in *The Man With The Donkey* (Hodder & Stoughton, London, 1965).